BALZAC'S OMELETTE

BALZAC'S OMELETTE

A delicious tour of French food and culture with Honoré de Balzac

ANKA MUHLSTEIN

Translated from the French by Adriana Hunter

OTHER PRESS

New York

Production Editor: Yvonne E. Cárdenas
Book design: Cassandra J. Pappas
This book was set in 12.25 pt. Fournier MT by Alpha Design & Composition
of Pittsfield, NH.

10 9 8 7 6 5 4 3 2

Library of Congress Cataloging-in-Publication Data
Muhlstein, Anka.
    [Garçon, un cent d'huîtres, Balzac et la table. English]
    Balzac's omelette : a delicious tour of French food and culture with Honoré
de Balzac / Anka Muhlstein ; translated from the French by Adriana Hunter.
        p. cm.
    Includes bibliographical references.
    ISBN 978-1-59051-473-3 (hardcover : alk. paper) — ISBN 978-1-59051-
474-0 (ebook) 1. Balzac, Honoré de, 1799-1850—Criticism and interpre-
tation. 2. Gastronomy in literature. 3. Food habits—France—History. I.
Hunter, Adriana. II. Title.

    PQ2178.M8413 2011
    843'.7—dc23

                        2011030790

For Louis

Contents

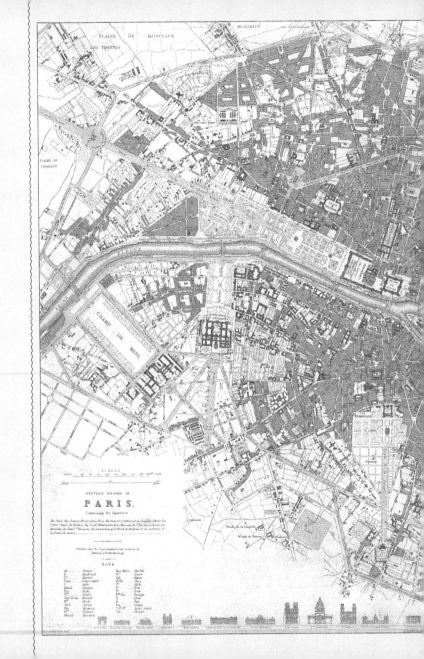

PLAINE DE MONCEAUX

MONCEAUX

LES TERNES

PLAINE DE
CHAILLOT

CHAMP DE MARS

SCALES

WESTERN DIVISION OF

PARIS.

Containing the Quartiers

Published under the Superintendence of the Society for the
Diffusion of Useful Knowledge.

NOTE

SCALES

EASTERN DIVISION
OF
PARIS.
Containing the Quartiers

Chronology

1799 Birth of Balzac in Tours on May 20. Napoleon, following a coup d'état, becomes first consul at the head of a new French government, putting an end to the Directory regime (1795–1799), which had been established under the constitution enacted by the Revolutionary Convention (1792–1795). The Consulate lasted from 1799 to 1804.

1804 Napoleon crowns himself emperor at the Notre-Dame Cathedral in Paris on December 2. The period of the First Empire lasts until June 1815, with an interruption from April 1814 to March 1815.

1812   Napoleon invades Russia. The campaign will end after six months. The French suffer devastating losses.

1814   Paris falls in March to the anti-French coalition of Russia, Prussia, Austria, Sweden, and England.

Napoleon abdicates in April; the Bourbon king, Louis XVIII, is restored, and Napoleon is exiled to Elba, an island between Corsica and northwestern Italy.

Balzac comes to live in Paris with his parents, two sisters, and younger brother.

1815   Napoleon escapes from Elba on March 1 and lands in France. The army rallies to him. Louis XVIII flees to Ghent on March 20. Napoleon regains control of the government but faces the same enemy coalition. On June 18 he is defeated at Waterloo and the Hundred Days of his return to power ends. With Napoleon exiled to St. Helena, Louis XVIII is restored for the second time.

1815–19   Balzac studies law and works in an attorney's office.

1822–25   Balzac writes mediocre novels under various pseudonyms. He starts a publishing company, then enters the printing business with borrowed funds. Financial success eludes him.

1822 Victor Hugo publishes his first volume of verse.

1824 Death of Louis XVIII. He is succeeded by his brother, Charles X.

1829 Balzac publishes *Les Chouans* under his own name. For the next twenty years he will publish each year novels, short stories, and articles.

1830 Charles X is overthrown by the July Revolution. His cousin, Louis-Philippe, Duke of Orleans, is crowned king of the French.

Stendhal publishes *The Red and the Black*.

1832 Balzac meets the love of his life, the Polish countess Madame Hanska.

Death of Sir Walter Scott, considered by Balzac to be his only rival.

1835 Publication of *Father Goriot*, the first book in which Balzac uses characters who have appeared in his previous works. This practice will continue throughout what will become *The Human Comedy*.

1841 Death of Count Hanski. Balzac and Madame Hanska are free to travel together. They visit Russia, Germany, Italy, and spend some time together in Paris, but will be separated for long periods of time.

1847 Balzac spends several months with Madame Hanska in Poland. In preparation for their marriage, he buys a house in Paris.

1848 A revolution in February forces Louis-Philippe to flee to England. The Second Republic is established. In December, Louis-Napoleon, the nephew of Napoleon I, is elected president.

1849 The French Academy rejects Balzac's candidacy. He travels to Poland.

1850 Balzac marries Madame Hanska on March 14 and returns with her to Paris in May.

He dies on August 18. Victor Hugo pronounces a superb graveside eulogy at the Père-Lachaise cemetery.

BALZAC'S
OMELETTE

INTRODUCTION

$\mathcal{D}$epending on how a Balzac text is interpreted, various unifying threads can be detected, threads chosen by the author as he carried out his studies of behavior. The most tenuous is a glove, the most common and robust money, and the most unexpected food.

Tell me where you eat, what you eat, and what time of day you eat, and I will tell you who you are. This utterly original preoccupation has no precedent among previous novelists. Do we picture the Princess of Cleves dunking a finger of bread into her boiled egg? It never occurs to Laclos to describe Madame de Merteuil's supper menu. A novelist as attentive to detail as Jane Austen takes more interest in the pattern on a plate than the food on it. On the other hand, you only need a whiff of the appalling, watery bean soup made by Madame Marneffe's maid in *Cousin Betty* to gauge how negligent she is in her role as mistress of the house, while the aroma from the hearty limpid stock that Jacquotte serves her master in *The Country Doctor* implies a perfectly run household. White stock is a sign of thriftiness, but only a miser of Monsieur Grandet's scope would give orders to make stock from a crow.

Balzac goes way beyond interiors. His era saw the advent of restaurants, and he plunged eagerly into this inexhaustible source of new material. Balzac's characters are defined as much by the café they choose, and their regular eatery or restaurant, as by their voice, their behavior, and their clothes.

Interestingly, Balzac was the first to understand the advantages of taking gastronomy into account in fiction. This distinguishes him from his immediate contemporaries: Victor Hugo, like Charles Dickens, uses food—or rather the lack of it—only to evoke the horrors of poverty; Anthony Trollope's characters never go to restaurants; the men go to their clubs where roast beef reigns supreme, and the women stay at home. George Sand essentially takes pleasure in describing rural meals that are more idyllic than realistic. But the next generation, starting with Flaubert, then Maupassant and more particularly Zola, spend as much time in the kitchen as they do in the living room. It is no coincidence that Zola, who set himself the task of handling all the great social themes of his age, devotes an entire volume of the Rougon-Maquart series to Les Halles, *The Belly of Paris*. And rightly so. In the nineteenth century Paris became the gastronomic capital of Europe. For people in all walks of life, food became an obsession, and Balzac was the first to consider this phenomenon—an admirable subject for the major bourgeois novelist that he was, constantly preoccupied with money, because a meal is both a costly and an ephemeral pleasure and a time when the most searing avarice and the most openhearted generosity may be revealed.

His preoccupation with all things gastronomic is first and foremost social, and this is endorsed by the fact that his characters spend hours on end in dining rooms, that his cooks' habits are described in detail, and that he gives the addresses of the best suppliers. And yet he is not concerned with how things taste. If you want to imagine savoring an oyster as it melts on your tongue, read Maupassant; if you dream of jugs filled with yellow cream, try Flaubert; and if the thought of beef in aspic tickles you, turn to Proust. But if you are interested not so much in the taste of the oyster as in the way a young man orders it, less the cool sweetness of the cream than how much it costs, and less the melting quality of the aspic than what it reveals about how the household is run, then read Balzac.

Nevertheless, as if to prove that food is not mere sustenance, Balzac's evocation of foodstuffs becomes an element of his style. An appetizing young peasant girl is a ham, a pale and wrinkled old woman looks like calves' sweetbreads. Gobseck, the aging moneylender whose patience withstands every test, is reminiscent of an oyster latched onto its rock. A girl's innocence "is like milk, which is turned by a thunderclap, by an evil smell, by a hot day, or even by a breath." Citing something as commonplace as an egg to evoke the satin whiteness of the nape of a neck or a pumpkin to depict a simpleton's face, describing a conversation that simmers away like thick broth or a smug character sprawling like a sturgeon on a fishmonger's stall, attracts the reader's attention. On the subject of the young Duke of Hérouville, whom Balzac finds woefully starchy, he says, "'It is good wine, but so tightly corked up that you break your corkscrews.'" Comparisons involving foodstuffs are never dry but as subtle and complex as the taste of a piece of fruit. The hapless Madame Grandet, crushed by her miserly husband, is like a mealy fruit that has lost all its flavor and juiciness. The nasty Mademoiselle Rogron in *Pierrette* is all avarice, avidly grasping things with her lobsterlike claws. And Delphine de Nucingen, such a washed-out creature with her white eyelashes, is compared to a Cox's pippin, an apple with blotchy markings like a frog, while the wicked Marquise d'Espard is a delicious little apple that warrants biting into. By contrast, only the juiciest, most sought-after fruit can evoke the cool shoulders of Madame de Mortsauf, the lady of the manor in *The Lily of the Valley*, or Madame Marneffe's firm breasts. The connection between fruit and desire pervades the novelist's work.

The surprise created by the very incongruity of these comparisons makes them remarkably effective. Maupassant went on to use the same technique blithely, particularly in *Ball-of-Fat*—the story of a kind, promiscuous girl who was "like a barrel of lard, her bloated fingers strangulated at the joints, like bunches of stubby sausages"—and Zola pushes it to extremes in *The Belly of Paris* when he describes Louise Méhudin, the magnificent fish seller who exhales "the bland smell of salmon, the musky violet of smelts, the acrid odor of herring and skate . . . her swinging skirts gave off their own mist; she walked in a cloud of evaporated sludgy seaweed . . . With her great goddess's body [she was] like a beautiful ancient marble statue rolled around by the sea and brought back to the shore in the nets of a sardine fisher." Flaubert was to do things slightly differently. He does not, for example, compare Charles Bovary to an item of food but describes the way he drinks his soup—always the same way, making the same noises, and demonstrating his satisfaction with the same gestures—to imply the full weight of boredom emanating from his person.

Balzac does not restrict himself to characters. Landscapes inspire him to the same metaphors, and he admits that the Touraine region reminds him of being up to his chin in pâté de foie gras. Paradoxically, this man, who is so keenly aware of the importance of food, was not a great food lover but the most eccentric of eaters. He barely ate anything for weeks on end during periods of intensive writing, then celebrated sending off the manuscript by abandoning himself to vast excesses of wine, oysters, meat, and poultry.

How to reconcile these contradictions? Quite simply by acknowledging that Balzac and his characters never ate at the same time: either he did or they did. Let us start with him and try to understand the importance he gave to food and the set pieces involving it in *The Human Comedy*.

I

BALZAC AT MEALTIMES

Balzac put too much of himself into his work not to leave us wondering how important food was to him, and this is no simple matter because he had the most unusual eating habits. Judging by portraits of him with his protruding stomach, and by his descriptions of various meals, how can we fail to imagine he was insatiably greedy, with a boundless appetite and a constant lust for food? Léon Gozlan, a friend, had fun describing him at mealtimes: "[His] lips quivered, his eyes lit up with delight, his hands shook with pleasure on seeing a pyramid of pears or beautiful peaches. There would not be a single one left to go and describe the defeat to the rest. He devoured the lot. He was a magnificent example of vegetal

Pantagruelism, tie whipped off, shirt open, knife in hand . . . [he] laughed explosively, like a bomb . . . then his chest would swell and his shoulders would dance beneath his jubilant chin . . . We thought we were seeing Rabelais at the Manse of Thélème Abbey. He melted for joy." We should not be too hasty with our conclusions. Balzac was no ordinary eater, and constantly swung from excess to frugality. He had practiced this frugality throughout his childhood and the better part of his youth. As an adult, he remained convinced that sobriety was necessary to an artist, but once the work was done, the stomach reaffirmed its rights.

Through imagination we can attain things that life has not offered us. Food was poor in the Balzac household, and the young Honoré never had an opportunity to pick his way around a kitchen full of delicious smells, to lift the lid on tempting pots and pans, or to watch a cake rising. Balzac the elder, whose ambition was to live to one hundred, ate only a piece of fruit as his evening meal at five o'clock and went to bed as early as possible. His wife, too preoccupied with her loves and her social life, "knew nothing of caresses, kisses and the pleasure of just being alive," and showed little concern for her eldest son Honoré's well-being. Balzac was not a spoiled child. His mother did not love him, at least he was convinced this was the case, and his mother's coldness colors all his childhood memories. It is true that even at a time when children had a tough upbringing, he does appear to have been particularly neglected as a child.

Honoré was sent away to a wet nurse when he was born, on May 20, 1799, and was already four years old when he came back to the family home. At eight he was packed off again to attend a boarding school in the Vendôme region. For six whole years he did not return home, in keeping with a rule laid down by the headmaster; this rule, inherited from the Oratorians who had run the establishment before the French Revolution, stipulated that families should not withdraw their children for the entire duration of their schooling. Of course they had every right to come and visit, but Balzac's parents, living in Tours, less than forty miles away, came to see their boy only twice. During this long period spent boarding, food was more a source of humiliation than of pleasure for the young schoolboy. The pupils ate little and badly in the refectory, with very few fresh vegetables and a couple of ounces of meat or a slender portion of salted fish per day. The parents knew this because, as with all schools, most of them arranged to supplement the diet. A normal mother would send parcels of jam, chocolate, or biscuits to her child, or allow him to buy what he needed or wanted in the canteen. Honoré was not privy to this sort of spoiling and, as he was given no pocket money, could not afford the delicacies that his classmates indulged in. He had no chance of participating in the food bartering organized by the children, and this contributed to his sense of isolation. He recalled this in describing the schooltime hardships of little Félix de Vandenesse in *The Lily of the Valley*:

The famous *rillettes* and *rillons* of Tours (a kind of sausage meat) formed the larger part of our midday luncheon, between breakfast in the morning and late dinner at the hour of our return home. This preparation, highly prized by some epicures, is rarely seen at Tours on any genteel table; though I may have heard of it before going to school, I had never been so happy as to see the brown confection spread on a slice of bread for my own eating; but even if it had not been a fashionable dainty at school, my longing for it would have been no less eager, for it had become a fixed idea in my brain . . . My school-fellows, almost all of the shopkeeper class, would come to display their excellent *rillettes*, and ask me if I knew how they were made, where they were sold, and why I had none. They would smack their lips as they praised their *rillons*, fragments of pork fried in their own fat and looking like boiled truffles; they took stock of my basket, and finding Olivet cheeses or dried fruit, struck me dumb by saying, "Why, you must really be poor!"

It was during these years at boarding school that Balzac, for want of food, became passionate about reading. Like the lonely schoolboy in *Louis Lambert*, another often biographical text, reading was for him "a sort of appetite which nothing could satisfy; he devoured books of every kind, feeding indiscriminately on religious works, history, philosophy, and physics . . . he found indescribable delight in reading dictionaries." With this unbalanced diet, which so accurately foretold the adult novelist, the young Balzac fell ill and returned to his family at the age of fourteen in a pitiful state. "He was struck down," his sister recalls in her memoirs, "by a sort of coma . . . Honoré had grown thin and sickly, he was like those sleepwalkers who sleep with their eyes open . . . No one in the family could forget the astonishment that the sight of Honoré produced when our mother brought him home from Vendôme. 'There,' our grandmother said in a pained voice, 'look at the state this school sends them home in, the pretty children we sent them.'" He recovered, thanks to his sisters' affection, fresh air, and a degree of liberty, although family tensions ran high. It was at this point that he probably grasped that the birth of his young brother Henry owed a great deal to the charms of a neighbor called Jean de Margonne, charms Honoré himself was sensitive to, for he formed a long and rewarding friendship with the man many years after Margonne had broken off with Madame Balzac. Honoré, who had poor relationships with his mother and brother, resumed the connection with Margonne during a trip to Touraine. From then on, whenever he needed peace and rest, he took refuge in the Château de Saché, the delightful home of this "family friend," which has now become a Balzac museum. When his old friends expressed surprise at this unexpected degree of intimacy, he would reply, "He owes me that at least," referring obliquely to the difficulties his unpleasant younger brother caused him.

In 1814, Balzac senior, who was a military provisions administrator, was posted to Paris, and the whole family left Tours to set up home in the Marais quarter. This was where Madame Balzac had previously lived with her parents, who made soft furnishings and embroideries on the rue Saint-Denis. It was a quarter full of small businesses, a large village where everyone knew everyone. The year 1815 saw the end of Napoleon's reign and, as a consequence, the end of Monsieur Balzac's administrative career. The restoration of the Bourbon kings—first Louis XVIII, then Charles X—almost inevitably saw a lot of managerial staff replaced. The Balzacs' social advancement came to an abrupt halt.

Honoré ended up boarding again at an institution on the rue de Thorigny, in a building that has now become the Picasso Museum. Once again, he suffered because he was unable to afford supplies from the porter, who, as was customary at the time, ran a canteen. Two years later he enrolled at law school and discovered everyday fare in students' restaurants; at seventeen, he took a post as a clerk in a firm of attorneys-at-law.

Balzac, at forty-three, after a daguerreotype by Nadar.

Here he familiarized himself with domestic dramas, the seeds of so many of his books; and here he experienced the happy, hectic, bantering lifestyle of his friends in the office. Being exuberant and irresistibly witty, Balzac entertained his colleagues so much that one day he received a note from the head clerk: "Monsieur Balzac is kindly requested not to come in today for there is much to do." It was the same then as it is now: young people are always hungry, and the clerks spent their time eating. Sitting on the marble mantelpiece of the condemned fireplace in the large dusty room where they worked were "diverse bits of bread, triangles of Brie cheese, fresh pork-chops, glasses, bottles, and a cup of chocolate for the head clerk. The smell of these comestibles amalgamated so well with the offensive odor of the over-heated stove and the peculiar exhalations of desks and papers that the stench of a fox would hardly have been perceived."

Balzac's disgust at the filth and the terrible smell of this food made a profound and lasting impression. He remembered it when, in *Father Goriot*, he described "the oilcloth which covers the long table so greasy that a waggish *externe* will write his name on the surface, using his thumb-nail as a style," the infernal clatter as boarders gathered around their leek soup, or Madame Marneffe's foul-smelling kitchen when she was destitute. Besides, how could anyone fail to notice that, in his imagination, a sumptuous meal is not so much an evocation of gastronomic pleasures as a display of luxury, a feast for the eyes just as much as it is for the mouth, if not more so. Eating for eating's sake always appalled him. He would rather eat an apple on his feet than sit down to a badly served meal. A dirty table napkin or an inadequately rinsed glass was enough to dull his appetite. When he traveled, he preferred to slip a smoked beef tongue and a dozen bread rolls into his bag and feed himself, rather than sitting at the stagecoach table in a post house to eat "the inn's ratatouilles," to use the young Oscar Husson's expression in *A Start in Life*, as he prepared for his first stagecoach trip, his pockets wisely filled with bread and chocolate by his mother.

Balzac did not stay shut away in the attorney-at-law offices for long. He managed to persuade his parents—who, when Monsieur Balzac retired, had had to leave Paris for the nearby village of Villeparisis—to give him two years to prove himself. Provided with a modest sum to ensure his survival, he found a home in the third-floor garret of a house on the rue de Lesdiguières, close to Bastille, where he lived from hand to mouth. These were not years of destitution—the fifteen hundred francs he was allocated per annum represented three times the average laborer's salary—but of work, solitude, and a very strict diet. He bought and cooked his own food, and described meals fit for a mouse to his sisters: a few sous' worth of milk, bread, and cherries, or bread and cheese (cheese was not really valued then and was thought of as poor man's food). If he was ever rash enough to buy a couple of melons one day, he had to settle for a handful of walnuts the next. Fruit seemed to constitute the mainstay of his diet. More importantly, he would go on to use these experiences several times in describing the early beginnings of young men destined to a glorious future, such as Desplein, the most illustrious surgeon in Paris, the feted master of Bianchon who would have died of starvation as a student had it not been for the generosity of his neighbor, a lowly water bearer; or the famous painter Joseph Bridau, who subjected himself to savage economizing in his youth in order to save his mother from poverty when she had been ruined by her eldest son. Balzac's conviction that work and excess were incompatible dates back a long way.

"I once used to live in a little street which probably is not known to you—the Rue de Lesdiguières. It is a turning out of the Rue Saint-Antoine, beginning just opposite a fountain near the Place de la Bastille, and ending in the Rue de la Cerisaie . . . I lived frugally, I had accepted the conditions of the monastic life, necessary conditions for every worker," he wrote in a novel bristling with autobiographical details. It cannot be said that these two years of privation brought forth a work of genius, far from it: he wrote *Cromwell*, a tragedy in five acts that his friends and family deemed so boring that he abandoned any attempt to have it staged. But Balzac would always refer to this trial as, if not beneficial, at least necessary for an artist. He illustrated this theory in *Cousin Betty* with the case of the sculptor Wencelas Steinbock, who produces admirable work so long as he is under the old maid's iron rule, because she keeps him concentrating on the job in hand, "kept by her in blinkers, as a horse is, to hinder it from seeing to the right and left of its road." But Steinbock surrenders to laziness and an easy life when he comes in contact with the riches and pleasures provided by his young bride, and his career then collapses. Material pleasures and "a woman's caresses scare away the Muse, and break down the sturdy, brutal resolution of the worker."

In 1820 Balzac abandoned his garret and threw himself into an active life, first writing the then equivalent of airport novels under a pseudonym, then trying his hand at various enterprises, and eventually earning a living writing novels, short stories, and articles. Unfortunately for him, he always earned less than he spent; until the day he died, this famous writer, one of the glories of French literature, lived in terror of the debtors' prison. But whether his financial circumstances were favorable or trying, his diet hardly changed: fasting in periods of intense work, "to avoid wearying the brain with digestion," and then, after creative periods, indulging in vast, shocking excess, comparable to sailors' binges after a long time at sea.

Balzac wrote quickly. Hounded by his creditors, spurred on by a fertile imagination, he closed the door and set himself to work for eighteen-hour days. Two months later the printer would receive the manuscript for *Father Goriot* or *Lost Illusions*. During these creative periods, he drank only water and coffee and sustained himself on fruit. Occasionally he took a boiled egg at about nine o'clock in the morning or sardines mashed with butter if he was hungry; then a chicken wing or a slice of roast leg of lamb in the evening, and he ended his meal with a cup or two of excellent black coffee without sugar. An ascetic then, our Balzac? In a sense, yes. But not always. Once the proofs were passed for press, he sped to a restaurant, downed a hundred oysters as a starter, washing them down with four bottles of white wine, then ordered the rest of the meal: twelve salt meadow lamb cutlets with no sauce, a duckling with turnips, a brace of roast partridge, a Normandy sole, not to mention extravagances like dessert and special fruit such as Comice pears, which he ate by the dozen. Once sated, he usually sent the bill to his publishers. Even alone at home, he could succumb to this sort of craving, particularly in periods of anxiety or sorrow, and in the space of fifteen minutes he could devour "a goose and a bit of chicory, with three pears and a pound of grapes," and, of course, made himself ill. A glutton then? Not that either. In Balzac's own words, a glutton "eats aimlessly, stupidly, soullessly . . . he eats things whole; they pass through his mouth without teasing his palate, without stirring the least thought; they head straight to oblivion in a frighteningly capacious stomach . . . nothing comes out of his mouth, everything goes in." No, that is not Balzac, who, in everyone's opinion, was the most amiable of guests, and what is more, had long periods of moderation. He had no trouble alternating between making do with swift meals and spending countless hours painstakingly tracking down the perfect ingredient.

His friend Léon Gozlan accompanied him on one macaroni hunt when this form of pasta was the height of fashion in Paris. Balzac had discovered a supplier on the rue Royale where they prepared the pasta by cooking it in the oven, while restaurants usually served it like a mini cannelloni, stuffed with meat, fish, or mushrooms. Coming out of a rehearsal at three o'clock in the afternoon—too late for lunch and too early for dinner—he ran from the boulevard des Capucines to the rue Royale and there "in three or four Gargantuan mouthfuls, laughing and praising Fenimore Cooper [whose *Pathfinder* he had just finished], he swallowed four helpings of pasta, to the stupefaction of the young lady in the shop." His friends said he was quite capable of scouring the whole of Paris to buy the best blend of coffee, a "knowing, subtle, divine decoction which was all his own like his genius. His coffee was made up of three types of bean: Bourbon, Martinique, and Mocha. He bought the Bourbon on the rue du Mont-Blanc [the present-day rue de la Chaussée d'Antin], the Martinique on the rue des Vieilles-Audriettes in the Third Arrondissement, and the Mocha in the faubourg St Germain on the rue de l'Université.

It was no less than a half day's expedition in search of a good cup of coffee." He was so fond of his own blend that he took it with him or had it sent when he went to stay at the Château de Saché, where the coffee was execrable, as it was throughout the countryside. Balzac was so incensed that coffee was neither infused nor filtered anywhere outside the capital that in a good many novels he deplores the barbarous habit of boiling it. In *The Peasantry*, for example, he describes the small town of Soulanges, some 125 miles from Paris, where the innkeeper "Father Socquard simply boiled [the coffee] in a large pipkin known in most households as 'the big brown pot.' He dropped in the mixture of powder and chicory, and, with an intrepidity which a Parisian waiter might have envied, served up the decoction forthwith in an earthenware cup which had nothing to dread from a fall on the floor."

It is widely known that Balzac drank large quantities of extremely strong coffee, not only to keep sleep at bay but also to sustain a state of excitement conducive to creativity. Thanks to coffee, he claimed, "ideas swing into action like battalions in the Great Army on a battlefield . . . Memories enlist at the double . . . and flashes of inspiration join the skirmish; faces take form; the paper is soon covered in ink." When he went to work in the middle of the night, he would make his own coffee in a Chaptal-style coffeemaker, the sort that Charles Grandet praises so highly to his cousin Eugénie, made of two receptacles separated by a filter. Over the years, he increased the concentration of his coffee, convinced that he could not write without the help of this drug, because that is precisely what coffee—"that cruel means of restoring mental agility"— had become for him. In the

The first percolators appeared in 1800. Balzac preferred this system to all others.

end, Balzac drank it by the potful, by the bucketful, despite the terrible cramps wringing his insides, the nervous eye twitches, and the burning in his stomach. Tea, he liked to think, could have replaced coffee, but he could not find any good enough. He complained of this to Madame Hanska, who sent him "caravan tea," her term for Chinese tea, from Poland. In exchange he obtained *cotignac* for her, a quince jelly that was extremely difficult to find. In order to satisfy this craving, he had to run around to every food supplier in Paris before tracking down the last box of it at Corcellet's, a gastronomic paradise newly opened at Palais-Royal. He needs no sympathy: this was exactly the sort of errand he relished.

Without further delay I must introduce Madame Hanska, Balzac's great love. In 1832 a stranger wrote him a letter so refined and so charming that he wanted to make her acquaintance. He met his correspondent, a Polish countess, in Geneva; he fell so violently in love with her that he made arrangements to see her again the following year. Notwithstanding her husband, they then spent an "unforgettable" night together and, in spite of the distance and the rarity of their meetings (they once went eight years without seeing each other), their relationship lasted and is documented by a correspondence of some two thousand pages, itself a source of many details about his everyday life. Once her husband was buried and her daughter married, Madame Hanska consented to marry Balzac. All that remained was to secure permission from the tsar, whose subject she was. The aging couple had to wait a few more years before the final authorization was obtained in 1850. They were married in March. Balzac died in August of the same year. But let us retrace our steps to the 1830s, a time of furious work, the first masterpieces, all-consuming debts, manic expenditure, and abundant coffee.

As soon as he had enough funds to do better than merely eat to sustain himself, and could invite a few friends to turn a meal into a pleasurable occasion, Balzac indulged his liking for scene setting. Naturally, excesses are more affordable when confined to the pages of a novel—hence the banker, Taillefer, in *The Magic Skin*, laying on a feast out of the *Thousand and One Nights*—but Balzac was not a man to begrudge expense in his personal life, particularly when he wanted to impress a lady. It was in this spirit that, one evening, he invited the ravishing Olympe Pélissier, a courtesan who had briefly granted him her favors. Olympe, a former model of Horace Vernet's, had been mistress to the successful novelist Eugène Sue before striking up a relationship with Rossini, whom she married in 1847.

Balzac invited her to a very small dinner of just five people, which caused him, he admitted to Madame Hanska, to provide "sumptuousness beyond reason. I have Rossini and Olympe, her cara dona who will preside . . . I have the most exquisite wines in Europe, the rarest flowers," but that was not all. He intended to serve salmon trout, chicken, then ice cream, and to present them on exquisite tableware. He went to the goldsmith Le Cointe (the same Le Cointe who made his celebrated walking stick with its turquoise-encrusted handle, which fueled the enthusiasm of caricaturists and inspired Delphine de Girardin's novel, *La Canne de M. de Balzac* [Monsieur de Balzac's Walking Stick]) and bought five silver plates, three dozen forks, and a fish slice with a lavish silver handle; once they had served their purpose, the entire collection had to go to the

Portrait of Countess Hanska, who married Balzac in 1850.

Mont de Piété pawnbrokers. The most astonishing illustration of his taste for ephemeral luxury is the meal he had delivered to himself in prison; yes, Balzac served a spell in prison, not for debts but for evading—several times—his duty to serve in the National Guard.

The Revolution of 1830 brought an end to the reign of the last Bourbon king, Charles X, and gave power to his cousin, the so-called citizen king, Louis-Philippe, thereby creating a less autocratic regime more favorable to the bourgeoisie. It was then decided that a National Guard should be set up, comprising taxable constituents and responsible for maintaining public order. Every citizen who lived in Paris had to mount the guard a few days a year, failing which he was condemned to a day's incarceration. Thinking this constraint intolerable, Balzac succeeded in avoiding it on numerous occasions, most often by claiming he was traveling or by simulating a house move: he would stay with a friend for a few days and wait for the danger to pass. Sometimes he did not escape in time but wriggled out of the tight spot by offering a few gold coins or a couple of good bottles of Vouvray to the arresting agents . . . until the day when he eventually had to submit to the law. Fearing they would lose their jobs if they did not bring back their prisoner this time, the law enforcers took him away on April 27, 1836. He was unceremoniously dumped at the Hôtel des Haricots, the National Guard's own prison on the rue des Fossés-Saint-Bernard. His valet, Auguste, had time to pack a suitcase for him with his quills, some paper, and the Dominican robe in which he liked to work. "You'll be able to work in peace here," the police officers had consoled him. But did Balzac want to be in peace?

Once he was settled in his third-floor cell, which looked out over a wine warehouse, he sent Auguste to his publisher Werdet with a note asking him to send money. Werdet complied immediately, and went to the prison armed with two hundred francs. To his considerable surprise, Balzac deemed the sum miserly but invited him in to dine. He had ordered a meal from Véfour, and explained to Werdet that he had deliberately chosen one of the most expensive restaurateurs in Paris because, on his release, he wanted to leave behind memories of "every tradition in the art of fine living." So down they went to the refectory at the agreed time and, at one end of a long table, they saw a magnificent meal set for two. It was theirs. The two friends enjoyed a succulent meal; Balzac proved in excellent humor when, at about seven o'clock, the door opened and another draft evader came in: Joseph-François Michaud, editor in chief of *La Quotidienne*, a royalist newspaper to which Balzac gladly contributed. Michaud eagerly accepted the invitation to share in Balzac's "modest" meal, and the evening ended in very high spirits, despite the presence, only a few chairs away, of a third prisoner, Eugène Sue, who was accompanied by two valets and haughtily refused to join them. There was nothing surprising about this coolness: relations between the two writers were not good. Sue, king of serialized works, was, according to Balzac, rich, cocooned from the real world, and never gave a moment's thought to literature. Balzac himself, with his constant concern for the quality of his writing, had trouble submitting to the rules of serialization, to chopping up his chapters and keeping his readers in suspense, as his contemporaries Eugène Sue and Alexandre Dumas so ably did. But he certainly would have liked the same revenue as his rivals, who were better paid than he. This particular episode was not yet over, though. The authorities decided to keep Balzac incarcerated a few extra days because he had several offenses to serve time for.

The following day, Werdet was therefore summoned and once more visited his author's cell. "His work table, his bed, his only chair, the entire floor of his room, everything was covered, everything was piled high, groaning with pâtés, stuffed poultry, glazed game, jams, baskets of different wines, and every sort of liqueur [from] Chevet. 'I don't want to go down to the refectory again,' Balzac explained, 'and meet that despicable fellow who answers to the name Eugène Sue, who never does anything for anyone else and has developed the most all-pervasive egotism." And so the editor and his author sat down to eat. As they could not possibly finish so many exquisite victuals and wines, Balzac decided to invite a few close friends to dinner. "Despite the prison's rules, the chief warder provided a large table, chairs, table linen and glasses. Auguste served us in white gloves. Nothing was missing. As he gave the signal for us to go into the gastronomic battle we were about to wage, Balzac repeated what he had said . . . claiming that this house (the euphemism he used for the prison) would always remember his stay there." There is no doubting his success in this, and the warders, who squabbled over the leftovers, celebrated their inmate's supreme indifference to waste and remembered him with fondness.

To ensure he avoided any further stays at the Hôtel des Haricots, Balzac decided to move officially to Sèvres, some three leagues (7.5 miles) from Paris, dispensing him from service altogether. Thanks to the railway, he could get from there to La Madeleine, a church in the center of Paris, in about twenty minutes for eight sous. When he needed to be in Paris full time, he hid in a small house in Passy (which is now the Balzac Museum), let by a man of straw or rather a woman of great heart, Louise de Brugnol, a respectable and energetic woman who could hold her own in tricky conversations with booksellers and could get rid of creditors who, despite every precaution, rang at the door. She acted as a governess and sometimes a cook to Balzac; she did not share his table at mealtimes but occasionally shared his bed. Balzac preached chastity to young authors as a way of preserving their creative drive, and bragged about it to his faraway idol; nevertheless, he also felt that total abstinence softened the brain. Madame de Brugnol permitted him to maintain a fruitful happy medium.

He had his correspondence sent to Sèvres, where he bought a succession of small plots of land, and started fixing up what he called his cabin, although this "cabin" required the services of "laborers, masons, painters and other workers." Once he had moved in, he happily received guests there, even during periods of intensive work. A great deal of drinking went on at Balzac's table, often too much. As his regular guest Léon Gozlan relates, "I won't name any names but I cannot help saying that, more than once, I've left presidents of the royal court well under the table." Balzac was more likely to stay on his feet, and, having only nibbled at his food, would leave the gathering early, at about seven o'clock, in order to get to bed so that he would be ready to start work at one o'clock in the morning.

In this instance, Balzac's sobriety is remarkable. I have always wondered why, despite this regimen, the man was so fat. He was not always that shape. Ten years earlier, he went to Brittany to stay with a family friend called Madame de Pommereul and flesh out his novel *The Chouans* (about the royalist insurrection during the Revolution and the Empire), and she took it into her head to fatten up this extremely thin and permanently hungry young man with plenty of craquelins* and butter. Balzac nicknamed her Lady Stuffing. She would not have recognized him in 1836, and he himself disliked his embonpoint; he forced himself to walk as much as possible to fight it, but how can anyone walk much when they work fifteen-hour days? And how did anyone walk in winter, in the Paris mud? At the time, only three streets had sidewalks, the rue de l'Odéon, the rue Louvois, and the rue de la Chaussée-d'Antin. Any weight he lost in summer reappeared as soon as

---

* In Brittany, craquelins are dry biscuits that may be either sweet or savory.

bad weather returned, despite his frequent resolutions to deprive himself of bread. It has to be said that his highly unusual diet—the dozens of pears eaten on a daily basis (he had fifteen hundred of them stored in his cellar in February, he told Madame Hanska one year), the huge quantities of grapes and the occasional binges—was not necessarily conducive to being slim. Still, it was possible that he would have found a degree of balance with Madame Hanska by his side, and Balzac himself certainly liked to think so when he talked to her of their future life together. Coming home one evening from a substantial dinner for twenty-five people given by James de Rothschild, where the food had not impressed him, he wrote her that he thought people would eat better at his table than with the rich and powerful: "In our house, we will never be more than nine at table. It is better to make seven people happy, to charm them, amuse them, listen to their wit and let them savor good fare than to feed them the way Véry* would." But significantly, in *The Human Comedy* characters do not always eat at home. And therein lies the novelty.

* Véry was the best restaurant in Paris at the time.

II

PARIS AT MEALTIMES

*T*here has never been a shortage of reasons to travel in France: gothic cathedrals, Norman churches, and royal châteaus are all attractions, but when all is said and done, star-hunting (by which I mean Michelin stars) is often the explanation for a *tour de France*. Measured against history, this is a new phenomenon. In the eighteenth century no one could have justified a trip to France for gastronomic reasons. Its people ate very badly. The high nobility and more refined townspeople were, of course, well served, their tables so prodigiously laden that guests consumed barely a third of what was offered (the surplus went first to servants, then to *regrattiers*, tradesmen who specialized in buying up leftovers). Few

Paris apartments had a real kitchen; an oven was a rare exception. Most housewives had to make do with a cauldron often precariously balanced in the hearth. Roasting spits were only to be found in inns or substantial houses.

Despite these limitations, before the Revolution people ate at home (unless they were traveling or staying in another town) and received guests at home. Meals were regarded as something private and, except in a few privileged households, menus could hardly be called exciting. These were tough circumstances for travelers from far afield who had no friends or letters of introduction, and found themselves at the mercy of unpleasant innkeepers: they complained as much about the rudimentary food as the general lack of comfort.

They had to settle for whatever badly cooked fare was put on the table, with no element of choice. At an inn, you bought not a particular dish but the right to sit at the communal table; another, scarcely better solution consisted in going to a table d'hôte, a sort of boardinghouse where regulars met at a set time. If there was an empty chair, the traveler could sit down; if not he had to try his luck elsewhere. There was never anything pleasant about the experience. According to Mercier, the author of *Tableau de Paris* (1788), the middle of the table, where the hostess put the most desirable dishes, was only accessible to regulars. Equipped with indefatigable jaws, they left only crumbs for the unfortunate visitor, who never ate as much as he had paid for and, on top of that, had to tolerate their noisy but vacuous conversations. The famous English agronomist Arthur Young complained particularly about this enforced proximity to louts.

The visitor often ended up buying a *saucisson* or a slice of ham from a charcuterie stall, or a cooked chop or chicken wing from a rotisserie, and eating it in his room. If he wanted a hearty stew, he had to go to a *traiteur,* who had the monopoly of ragouts and would deliver whole prepared meals. There were also lively street markets, where women made the most of an age-old privilege and set up shop behind a great cauldron of simmering tripe while their partners tended constantly steaming pots of cooked chicken. The whole arrangement was neither practical nor salubrious. The guilds imposed stringent rules on every kind of tradesman and determined very precisely what each of them could sell or cook, therefore forbidding anything resembling what we would call a restaurant, in other words a place where the customer can sit at an individual table and order a meal he or she has chosen, paying only for this chosen food. In fact, in the eighteenth century, the French word *restaurant** meant not an establishment but a food or

---

* The French word for "restore" is *restaurer*, hence the meaning of *restaurant* as "restorative."

The horrors of a table d'hôte.

drink with restorative qualities—a glass of wine, a cordial, or some reduced stock which was effectively essence of meat.

When in about 1780 a few unclassifiable establishments—neither grocers, inns, *traiteurs,* nor table d'hôtes—appeared in Paris as clean, discreet establishments where a lady could sit alone at a table covered with a cloth and order a bowl of stock or a salad, they were given the name *restaurants* because they seemed intended not to satisfy a major appetite but simply to offer passersby a pick-me-up, something restorative.

The first restaurant proper opened on the rue des Poulies (the present-day rue du Louvre); a few years later it moved to the Hôtel d'Aligre on the rue Saint-Honoré. The manager, whose name was Boulanger, served poached poultry with sea salt, fresh eggs, and, of course, highly concentrated stock. He could not serve stews but was exempted from the tough restrictions that imposed set mealtimes on table d'hôtes. The attraction of this new setup was that if someone felt a little tired during the course of the day, they could find something here to invigorate them. A rare few innovators followed this lead. There were only four or five restaurants in Paris before 1789. The most famous, Vacossin, played host to Jean-Jacques Rousseau, who described the dinner he had as a picnic,* implying that the fare was light and the bill split fairly.

Amongst many other things, the Revolution transformed the gastronomic landscape of Paris. It might seem frivolous to take an interest in the cuisine of an era scarred by violence, terror, murderous war, and scarcity culminating in 1794, but there are many factors that fully justify an interest in the subject: the astonishing parade of fine foods delivered to people in prison (those condemned to death made arrangements to have roasts and pâtés delivered by *traiteurs* and other suppliers, who

* The original French word *pique-nique* denoted a meal where everyone brought and/or paid for their own food.

made sure their cards were circulated around the dungeons); sumptuous public feasts; and, most significantly, a transformation of the entire industry of eating.

Three days after the storming of the Bastille, when the Prince of Condé fled into exile, he left behind an army of spit roasters, sauce makers, and pastry cooks who had all worked under orders from the chef, Monsieur Robert. The latter lost no time in opening a restaurant, which he called Robert, at 104 rue de Richelieu—a real restaurant with a varied menu, serving whatever he wanted. Regulations, some of which dated back to the Middle Ages, had just been slackened, and the primary beneficiaries were these newcomers, the restaurateurs. The head cook to the Comte de Provence, the king's brother, set himself up at the Galerie de Valois in the Palais-Royal as soon as the prince had left in June 1791, and unabashedly invited diners into this luxurious setting and offered them a doorstop-sized menu. The whole neighborhood was soon a meeting place for gastronomes . . . and there were hordes of them.

The nouveaux riches, who were plentiful because there was no shortage of opportunities to make money, had good appetites. But in these troubled times no one was keen to display their wealth—at least not before the post-Revolutionary regime, the Directory, was established. Setting up and running a household in grand style or laying oneself open to envy or denunciation by giving dazzling dinners would have been dangerous; it was better to invite and receive guests at a restaurant, where private rooms even offered a degree of discretion. Still more important: at the time, Paris thronged with single men, members of the Assembly, journalists, interested onlookers, and foreign observers. Many had no connections in the capital but still had to eat, hence the rush to these pleasant modern establishments with menus to suit every purse and meals at every hour of the day. The sheer convenience of this arrangement meant that restaurants opened in every quarter, and their numbers kept on growing. The movement expanded further under the Consulate and the Empire, and one English journalist, Francis Blagdon, who came to Paris once peace was restored in 1802, eager to see the result of more than ten years of war and revolution, described the capital in one word: restaurants. At the time, the accepted figure was two thousand establishments, a figure that rose again under the Restoration and reached three thousand. (Table d'hôtes had mostly disappeared or had adopted the current fashion by adding a few individual tables to their dining rooms and offering a choice of dishes.) One consequence of this phenomenon was that a new timetable was adopted, and this had a profound effect on the structure of the day for Parisians.

Before the Revolution, people in good society ate three times a day: they had something between six and eight in the morning, then dined at about two o'clock and supped after nine o'clock. Peasants and laborers made do with two meals. Supper was reserved for the privileged minority who went to balls or performances. During the Revolution, the system dissolved: all those men unleashed into the streets of Paris at the crack of dawn for discussions in the Assembly, clubs, and various societies, were collapsing by eleven o'clock . . . and eagerly headed for restaurants toward the end of the morning, which did nothing to stop them from wanting to eat again at about six o'clock in the evening. This late morning meal was then given the name *déjeuner*,* as compared to the *petit déjeuner* (little breakfast) eaten on rising, and the last meal of the day took on the name *dîner* (dinner). *Souper* (supper) all but vanished. This was a wonderful windfall for restaurateurs, who now benefited from two sittings a day.

From that point on, people took to gathering with friends and arranging to meet and eat in public places, and this was true of all social classes. It was a period in which cooking was granted incredible importance; it became the order of the day and remained so during the Empire and the following regimes. Gastronomy became a subject of conversation and even of literature. In the seventeenth century, two books of

---

* Literally "de-fast," like the English word "breakfast."

A supper to celebrate Saint Hubert, the patron saint of hunters, at the restaurant Véfour.

recipes—*Le cuisinier français* and *Les délices de la campagne*—had been all that housewives needed for generations, but these gave way to ambitious works by Cabanis and Brillat-Savarin, whose *La physiologie du goût*, a series of meditations on the art of eating, was prodigiously successful. Alexandre Dumas published a cookbook with witty illustrations, crammed with anecdotes and excellent recipes. France had become the homeland of great cooking. And Balzac, who depicted its times, its people, and its interests, appointed himself as a mouthpiece for this trend.

"If the French have as great an aversion to traveling as the English have a propensity for it," he said, "both English and French have perhaps sufficient reasons. Something better than England is everywhere to be found; whereas it is excessively difficult to find the charms of France outside France." And the essence of these French charms lay in its cooking; "as Borel [the great chef at Le Rocher de Cancale] elaborates it for those who can appreciate it . . . it is the wines of France, which . . . are to be regarded as myths." And Balzac had a tremendous time disparaging foreign cooking. Italy was the country where they put cheese in soup, he wrote disdainfully in *Gambara*, and Poland the one where there were seventy-seven ways of preparing gruel, not to mention their repulsive beet soup, *barksch** (Balzac perhaps chose this variant spelling because it comes close to the French word for "yuk"). The Germans, he claimed, liked different sorts of vinegar, collectively referring to them as Rhineland wines. As for the English, they needed fiery condiments to reawaken their taste buds.

$\mathcal{B}$ALZAC TAKES us all over Paris, on the right bank as much as the left, sending his characters off into the most refined establishments and the most lowly, and through his succession of novels gives us a real social and gastronomic report on the capital. Some forty restaurants are referred to in *The Human Comedy*, because he is not satisfied with mentioning only the biggest names. Whether discussing the most spectacular or the most modest, Balzac lingers over the menu. As is always the case with him, he is also interested in the cost. His work, therefore, amounts to a guide, one that discerns the stars but does not neglect the bill. Two restaurants in *The Human Comedy* warrant the full three stars: Véry and Le Rocher de Cancale. Let us start with the oldest, Véry, because it was here that Balzac took Lucien de Rubempré to be initiated into the joys and perils of Parisian life.

The ninth day of Thermidor* marked the end of Robespierre's reign and of the terrible excesses of the Terror. The guillotine with its cortege of executioners and victims was transferred from the place de la Concorde to the eastern outskirts of Paris. Parisians could start to breathe more freely. The Terrasse des Feuillants on the northern edge of the Tuileries Gardens, cut off from the road by a wall covered in arbors, was a delightful spot once more. It was here that, under the

---

* A new calendar, with new names for the days of the week and the months of the year, was adopted during the Revolution. The ninth of Thermidor, year II of the Republic, corresponds to July 27, 1794.

Directory, two brothers from the Lorraine region set up a magnificent restaurant that they called Chez Véry. Gastronomic purists occasionally criticized the fare for staying so classic and having little inclination for innovation, but the quality of the service, the luxurious décor, and—in particular—the profusion of mirrors attracted and dazzled customers. Véry had to move in 1801 when the rue de Rivoli was laid down. But it did not leave the neighborhood: it moved toward Palais-Royal to take over premises in the rue de Beaujolais which are now home to the restaurant Le Grand Véfour. Like other restaurants, Véry set out individual tables in the main room where columns afforded space between the tables. A movable screen could be used to divide up the room, and Véry went one step further by offering large groups or intimate twosomes private rooms where the waiter never entered without knocking.

Véry's fame was unstoppable. Russian officers coming into France with the 1814 invasion headed to the Palais-Royal at the gallop, crying "Véry, Véry." "As soon as a stomach arrives in Paris, that is the first table it wishes to visit, and it will return again and again. For it is quite sure that there, throughout the year, it can eat fish as fresh as in the sea, excellent game, trotters stuffed with truffles, white pudding and black pudding, papillotes of partridge with truffles, brains and even macaroni . . . Véry is the palace of all restaurants and the restaurant of palaces," according to a diners' guide from the Restoration. Hardly surprising then that the hero of *Lost Illusions*, the young poet Lucien Rubempré, who is reeling after a chilly rebuff from the woman who lured him to Paris, decides to go there to console himself. He has to demonstrate a degree of courage to venture into the best and most elegant restaurant in Paris fresh from his provincial home, when he ate in a restaurant for the first time only the day before. Lucien is so new to Paris that he has to ask the way to Palais-Royal, but he boldly "went to Véry's and ordered dinner by way of an initiation into the pleasures of Paris and a solace for his discouragement. A bottle of Bordeaux, oysters from Ostend, a dish of fish, a partridge, a dish of macaroni and dessert—this was the *ne plus ultra* of his desire. He enjoyed this little debauch, studying the while how to give the Marquise d'Espard proof of his wit, and redeem the shabbiness of his grotesque accoutrements by the display of intellectual riches. The total of the bill drew him down from these dreams, and left him the poorer by fifty of the francs which were to have gone such a long way in Paris. He could have lived in Angouleme for a month on the price of that dinner. Wherefore he closed the door of the palace with awe, thinking as he did so that he should never set foot in it again."

Balzac himself was often surprised by the extraordinary final sum of his bill at Véry's, but unlike his character, he had

A dandy studying the menu at Véry.

perfected a strategy. He gave a large tip, signed the bill, and had it sent to his publisher by Madame Véry (a tremendously buxom woman, if we are to believe a sketch by the English painter Rowlandson), who presided over the room behind her counter, keeping a watchful eye on waiters and customers while she swiftly totted up figures.

All the same, I wonder whether Balzac did not prefer Véry's great rival, Le Rocher de Cancale, which was more cheerful and modern with a more relaxed atmosphere, as is fitting for a restaurant in Les Halles, a neighborhood with a greater working-class population than Palais-Royal. And Le Rocher particularly distinguished itself for the quality of its oysters. Now Balzac—and in this he differed little from his contemporaries—seems to have had a real fixation for oysters. Louis XVIII often swallowed a hundred of them at the start of a meal while he was in refuge at Gand during the Hundred Days, the brief period in 1815 when Napoleon reclaimed power after his escape from Elba. As the dining room looked out over the street, the officer on duty had to shoo away street children who heaved themselves up to the windows to count how many platefuls the exiled king ate. It is therefore hardly remarkable that Balzac's characters consume them with such abandon. From a conversation reported in *The Duchess of Langeais*, we are not surprised to learn that the Count of Montriveau, in exile in Saint Petersburg, consoles himself by gulping down a hundred oysters a day, without suffering gout or gallstones as a result of these excesses. The pretty Coralie, wanting to please her lover Lucien, orders oysters with lemon for their first lunch, and in *César Birotteau* there is nothing peculiar about the fact that the hideous Claparon, the corrupt traveling salesman who lives in a hovel, still manages to eat oysters on a corner of his paper-strewn work desk. Being a true connoisseur, the rich middle-class Balthasar Claes, the unhappy hero of *The Quest of the Absolute*, always orders them directly from Ostend.

In Paris, the king of oysters was the first owner of Le

Rocher de Cancale, Alexis Balaine, who started out selling oysters in Les Halles, in the very heart of the fish market. It was a lucrative position. There was considerable demand for oysters in Paris, given that six million dozen were consumed a year. At the turn of the century, Balaine opened a restaurant on the corner of the rue Montorgueil and the rue Mandar; it was a good, second-tier establishment that attracted attention from connoisseurs, particularly Cambacérès, who was then second consul. The regime of the Consulate was instituted after the coup d'état of the eighteenth of Brumaire, when Napoleon Bonaparte seized power, and lasted from 1799 to 1804. Bonaparte, who had adopted the title of first consul, actually governed; Cambacérès, who was a legal specialist, and Lebrun, the third consul, who was in charge of financial affairs, both aided him but only had consultative powers. Cambacérès's patronage could make a great difference for a restaurant because the excellence of his table was so well documented. One anecdote claims that, in 1801, enraged by an order from Bonaparte to reserve the postal service specifically for dispatches, he went straight to the first consul to protest, saying, as the rumor has it: "How do you expect us to make friends if we do not offer them sought-after delicacies? It is through food that one governs." Confronted with such indignation, Bonaparte gave in to him and allowed him to continue taking delivery of turkeys stuffed with truffles from the provinces, pâté from Strasbourg, hams from Mayence, and his rock partridges, which he so preferred to the gray variety.

Soon the Société des Épicuriens (Epicurean Society) started holding their dinners there. Le Rocher de Cancale was launched, prices soared, and it sustained its reputation for many years. Balaine fine-tuned an exceptional menu and perfected stunning lighting but continued to offer the most simple dishes: ham with spinach, vol-au-vent pastries with cream, and, of course, oysters, all year round, always of the finest quality, even in stifling weather. In Balzac's day, Balaine had already retired and sold his business to Borel (who had been tutored by one of the Prince de Condé's former chefs) for 170,000 francs, a very considerable sum, equivalent to the dowry for a daughter of a marshal of the Empire, but this did the restaurant no harm at all. Balzac granted it preference, as is proved by the invitation he sent to one of his admirers, a young Russian called Monsieur de Lentz. The latter had insisted most vigorously that he wanted to meet him, Balzac reported to Madame Hanska. He eventually yielded and organized a dinner at Le Rocher with his friend Léon Gozlan and Victor Hugo, whom he invited with these words:

My dear Master, I wish to speak to you and, as this entails a dinner to be had at the Rocher de Cancale this Thursday, take on no engagements and reserve your evening for me; I shall come to explain the above tomorrow morning, Wednesday.

With my heartfelt regards,

. . .

There will be only one Russian who adores you, Léon Gozlan and myself.*

Sadly, we know nothing of the menu, except that Balzac and Lentz nibbled on the odd prawn and radish while waiting for Hugo. They were welcomed most considerately by Borel, who looked after them as well he knew how for his most famous customers, and were seated before the most sumptuous and appetizing of spreads, where "the beauty of each piece, all braised and garnished, their freshness, their cleanness created a ravishing sight."

The present-day equivalent of Le Rocher de Cancale would be a cross between Le Taillevent, the most highly reputed restaurant in Paris, and a large, varied, and bustling brasserie like La Coupole, with incomparable dishes and an

---

* Madame Hugo scribbled on Balzac's letter: "No point replying, I've taken you on."

interesting clientele in which politicians, journalists, writers, editors, actors, and high society all rub shoulders. It is hardly surprising that Balzac sends the whole of his Human Comedy there, some for a lover's meal, others for business meetings, late-night suppers with courtesans, or society dinners, from 1815 right through to 1845, when the restaurant closed.* De Marsay goes there to quell his impatience and "drank like a fish, ate like a German" while waiting for his appointment with the mysterious Paquita; notary clerks gather here for a blowout feast that starts at three o'clock but does not end till ten! It is here that, in *Lost Illusions*, du Châtelet brings Madame de Bargeton, the great lady newly arrived from the provinces with her young lover, Lucien de Rubempré, the very evening of their arrival, in order to make sure the lady understands his standing as an elegant Parisian who feels "quite in his element [there]. He smiled at his rival's hesitations, at his astonishment, at the questions he put, at the little mistakes which the latter ignorantly made, much as an old salt laughs at an apprentice who has not found his sea legs." Knowing how to order from "waiters, whom a provincial might have taken for diplomatists but for their age, [who] stood solemnly, as knowing themselves to be overpaid," and leafing confidently through a menu, re-

---

* It reopened two years later across the street under new ownership, but never regained its former reputation.

quired a certain savoir-faire that Lucien quickly learned when he started spending time with actresses—rather more cheery and indulgent guides than du Châtelet, who so longs to humiliate him.

It has to be said that the endless menu, which was printed in four columns of small print, could have been mistaken for *Le Moniteur Universel*, the government's official newspaper. Like Véry, Borel offered over one hundred dishes. Veal alone could be ordered roasted, fried, stuffed with peas, as a blanquette, a fricandeau, or a plate of sliced meat, and as medallions, brains, marinated ear, head, tongue, sweetbreads, or chops. (We should not forget that the restaurateur often bought the whole carcass and was therefore impelled to sell not only the noble cuts, such as loin and rib, but the entire animal.) On top of this, the vocabulary, which was inherited from great houses where chefs had done their apprenticeship before the Revolution, was often impenetrable to the uninitiated. Was it better to order Toadstone Pigeon or "invest" in Pigeon à la financière? What on earth could an epigram of lamb be? How to choose between sauces that called themselves Hollandaise, German, Spanish, Italian, Bavarian, à la pluche, à la barigoule, and à la Robert?

This nomenclature continued to produce astonishment for a long time, according to Flaubert. Is it a political gesture to refuse a "Pudding à la d'Orléans" and should legitimists order their turbot "à la Chambord"?* To facilitate diners' choices, a journalist called Honoré Blanc had the idea of collating menus from twenty-one restaurants, and translating them into simple French so that all apprentice gastronomes could order their meals without making fools of themselves in front of head-waiters who were far more familiar with the terms than their nouveaux riches customers.

Nevertheless, despite difficulties in choosing a meal, every-one was flattered to be invited to Le Rocher de Cancale. In *The Muse of the Department*, Dinah invites her lover there to soften the blow of her decision to leave him; in *Lost Illusions*, the awful Vautrin makes the most of an exquisite dinner to per-suade the young courtesan Esther to obey him blindly; Baron Hulot takes Valérie Marneffe there again and again to win her favor in *Cousin Betty*. Even the Duchess of Maufrigneuse, who is too refined to go to restaurants, is intrigued by Le Rocher: "she liked anything amusing, anything improvised. Bohemian restaurants lay outside her experience; so d'Esgrignon [the young man wooing her] got up a charming little party at the Rocher de Cancale for her benefit, asked all the amiable scamps

---

* Louis-Phillipe, Duke of Orléans, replaced his cousin Charles X on the French throne after the 1830 Revolution. Charles's grandson, the Comte de Chambord, and his followers considered the Orléans usurpers.

whom she cultivated and sermonized, and there was a vast amount of merriment, wit, and gaiety, and a corresponding bill to pay." Despite the pretty Diane's clearly demonstrated independence of mind, Balzac spares her from witnessing the final ending of *Cousin Betty*. At Le Rocher de Cancale that particular evening, "ravishing women walked through the dining room towards a large private room, their satin gowns trimmed with English lace in such quantities it would have fed an entire village for a month, wearing rare flowers in their hair and decked in pearls and diamonds." Gathered around a table decorated with the silver service that Borel reserved for this sort of feast and under streaming lights, the noisy, laughing courtesans, surrounded by admirers, tucked into oysters and, still chattering and joking, started in on soups, poultry, pâtés, fish, and roast meats. What are we to think of the forty-two bottles consumed by fourteen diners? The figure seems unrealistic and yet, throughout the century, whether people ate alone, with one other person, or in groups, they drank heavily. Flaubert finds nothing remarkable in pointing out that in *A Sentimental Education*, Arnoux, the middle-class Parisian, and Frédéric, the provincial young student, order a bottle of Sauternes, a bottle of Burgundy, some champagne, and liqueurs at lunchtime. True, when Frédéric arrives home, even though he has drunk less than his companion, he feels he needs a siesta.

Théophile Gautier once saw Balzac celebrate sending a manuscript off to his editor by downing "four bottles of Vouvray white wine, one of the most intoxicating known to man and [which] did nothing to alter his sturdy mind and only served to add an extra sparkle to his gaiety." Wine did not have the least effect on him, perhaps, he thought, because of his long-standing habit of drinking coffee. All the same, Balzac did admit to being a "costly guest."

So people drank a great deal at the time, and very rarely water. The only characters in *The Human Comedy* who drink nothing but water are the writer Daniel d'Arthez, the very picture of the idealistic artist, and the Marquise d'Espard, an inveterate coquette who wants to preserve her youthful looks. Balzac mentions one other man who drinks water, but he does so in very specific circumstances described in *The Red Inn*. In this passage, the banker Taillefer is at a dinner and hears another guest telling the story of a mysterious murder. As far as Taillefer is concerned, there is no mystery at all because the murderer is none other than himself. In his nervous state, he knocks back two whole carafes of water in quick succession, thereby awaking suspicions. Finally, at the end of *The Splendors and Miseries of Courtesans*, when Vautrin is reeling with concern about Lucien's fate, he drinks a tub of water in his cell at the Conciergerie. In Balzac's world, drinking a glass of water is never a natural gesture, it is a clue.

Balzac has too much fun at Le Rocher through his characters to give the same weight to the other great restaurants. He does, however, refer to Frères-Provençaux (Provence Brothers), whose owners, three cousins in fact, came up to Paris during the Revolution and moved into premises very close to Palais-Royal, on the rue Helvétius (now the rue Sainte-Anne), opposite the rue Louvois. On tables covered with oilcloths, they introduced Provence cuisine to Parisians, who delighted in their bouillabaisse and their brandades. After the terrible years of Robespierre's reign, the Brothers moved to the galerie de Beaujolais and, although the prices were more modest than in the most famous restaurants, the cuisine matched theirs. But Balzac does not linger there long and sends only unsympathetic characters to eat there, such as Félix de Vandenesse's parents or the fake banker, the loathsome Claparon, who contributes to the ruin of César Birotteau, the honest perfumer brought down by his own credulity. The restaurant may well have been excellent, but in the Balzac guide, the Brothers do not warrant the stars of high repute. Nevertheless, the place continued to thrive, and Flaubert's Arnoux was still eating there in 1848, complaining all the while that its food was not as impeccable as it once had been. What Balzac really did not like, in fact, was the Palais-Royal neighborhood.

It seems that from 1830 onward fashionable people actually started tiring of the district. Men might, for example, still meet at Grignon's for lunch, but these lunches were more ostentatious than elegant and always disintegrated into drunken scenes. This was clearly a bad sign for the area. Somehow, Palais-Royal (which had been the belly of pleasure and business throughout the eighteenth century, with is galleries lined with shops, cafés, restaurants, gaming houses, and discreet brothels) had become unpleasant and even, in places, sinister. Esther, one of the famous courtesans of *The Human Comedy*, lives there for a while on the rue de Langlade, a "narrow street, dark and muddy . . . [that] wears at night an aspect of mystery full of contrast." In *Gambara*, Balzac has his hero walk along the rue Froidmanteau, "a dirty, poky, disreputable street—a sort of sewer tolerated by the police close to the purified purlieus of the Palais-Royal, as an Italian majordomo allows a careless servant to leave the sweepings of the rooms in a corner of the staircase. The young man hesitated. He might have been a bedizened citizen's wife craning her neck over a gutter swollen by the rain." Balzac uses the word *bourgeoise* for this "citizen's wife," and the word is chosen deliberately: the shamelessness and vice around Palais-Royal displeased the burgeoning bourgeoisie.

The Boulevard des Italiens, the most fashionable thoroughfare of Paris.

From then on, the boulevard des Italiens—the thoroughfare that "anyone who was anyone crossed at least once a day"—became fashionable. In an article about new neighborhoods, Balzac enthuses: "The boulevards are now to Paris what the Grand Canal was to Venice . . . the Corso to Rome . . . the Graben to Vienna . . . that is, where freedom of intelligence is to be found, and life itself." It was the site of choice for the great cafés, Hardy's on the corner of the rue Lafite, Riche's on the corner of the rue Peletier, as well as the Café de Paris and the Café des Anglais. Of course, these "cafés" were restaurants, but new-wave restaurants, not as serious as the former greats of Palais-Royal that focused so intently on gastronomy. These were restaurants where cool counted for more than cost. People went there to be seen rather than to have a delectable meal, although the food was excellent at the Café des Anglais. The latter had the added advantage of having twenty-two private rooms. It is not surprising then that the pretty Delphine de Nucingen, who takes little persuasion to cheat her fat banker of a husband with the latest young men, has access to the place. It is from here that she orders a dinner to be delivered to the bachelor apartment she has just set up for her new lover Eugène de Rastignac. A few years later, Rastignac becomes a regular at the establishment, and is often seen there with the king of dandies, Henri de Marsay. While the cooking may have been discernibly worse at the Café de Paris, the decor was very refined, the furnishings were comfortable, the silverware was always gleaming, and this was where wealthy young things liked to be seen. They were happy to spend time there.

One of the great cafés is conspicuous by its absence in *The Human Comedy*: the Café Hardy, the place that introduced the *déjeuner à la fourchette* (fork lunch), so named because a waiter would stand in front of a large buffet and use a long fork to reach for the cold cuts pointed out by each customer. Indeed, when it opened during the Revolution, the owner, Madame Hardy, served no hot food. Her lone male customers ate oysters, tripe, cold meats, and pâtés from about eleven o'clock in the morning. Interestingly, salads were available, but no vegetables were served. For dessert there were table creams, charlottes, and ice creams. Then, when lunch became a more important meal under the Empire, Madame Hardy set up a large grill beside the buffet displaying her wares. Customers looked on while the headwaiter cooked breaded pigs' trotters with truffles, kidneys or chicken fillets served with the "fires of hell," which meant covered in a layer of salt and pepper strong enough to take the roof off your mouth. But, to its great regret, Hardy's, which was wildly successful under the Empire, never established itself as an evening restaurant. It did not recover from its founder's retirement, and lost much of its standing during the Restoration. It was relaunched many years later, in 1839, under the name Maison Dorée, a mixed establishment that was often frequented by women best described as escorts and where any respectable woman would be offended to be invited.

Lunch now became a meal that was highly prized by the young. Good manners dictated that this meal should not be taken too seriously, although it had become very substantial. In an article published in *La Mode*, Balzac advocated a sort of gracious disorder for lunch. Demonstrating too much elegance at this particular meal was the height of vulgarity. In *The Unconscious Comedians*, Sylvestre Gazonal, a lace maker recently arrived in Paris from the eastern Pyrenees on a business trip, is invited to lunch by his cousin, the fashionable painter Léon de Lora. The provincial guest makes the mistake of wearing his bright blue suit with gold buttons over a shirt with a jabot and a white waistcoat, as well as yellow gloves. Worse still, he commits the blunder of arriving early. Lunching at ten is considered ridiculous in Paris, the headwaiter points out to him: gentlemen here lunch between eleven o'clock and noon. Lora and Bixiou, his caricaturist friend, duly arrive at half past eleven, wearing whatever came to hand, according to Gazonal. They have a "monster" of a meal, "in the course of which they consumed six dozen Ostend oysters, half a dozen cutlets à la Soubise, chicken à la Marengo, a lobster mayonaise [*sic*], mushrooms on toast, and green peas, to say nothing of *hors d'oeuvres*, washed down with three bottles of bordeaux, three of champagne, several cups of coffee and liqueurs." Gazonal was less impressed by the food than by the quantity of gold coins handed over in payment. He even noticed the tip the waiter was given, thirty sous, a day's wages for a laborer, he pointed out to his friends back home in the country.

At the Café Riche, customers were less casual—at least they were in Balzac's day, for thirty years later, in Zola's books,

The kitchen of the Café Riche.

drunken courtesans would be smearing obscenities on the mirrors in the private dining rooms. A contemporary engraving gives an impression of this huge establishment (all that remains of it today is the smaller Petit Riche, whose decor has not changed and which originally served a more modest clientele). In one corner of the enormous kitchen was a roasting rack easily wide enough for six spits, in another a meat larder in which rabbits, partridges, and pheasants hung; in the middle stood an oven with a good dozen cooks working around it. There were two fish tanks for keeping lobster and fish; in front of them were two long tables for the pastry chefs putting together desserts and waiters preparing platefuls of food. There were shelves all around the walls for dishes and jars, and on the floor were barrels of anchovies, sardines, and pickles. Lastly, saucepans and casserole dishes were hooked onto rails hanging from the ceiling. In the middle of this bustle stood three stern figures in black garb, directing the constant flow of waiters. People did not go to the Riche to show off, as they did at the Café des Anglais or the Café de Paris, but to eat, and they very quickly became regulars.

In *The Muse of the Department*, the impoverished journalist Etienne Lousteau has improbably seduced Dinah de la Baudraye, who abandons her château and her husband the baron to join him in Paris; the couple eat in one of its private dining rooms every evening until the day the baroness realizes the exorbitant cost of this treat:

"Dearest heart," said she, "finish your novel without making any sacrifice to necessity; polish the style, work up the subject.—I have played the fine lady too long; I am going to be the housewife and attend to business." . . .

"Well, it makes very little difference to us whether we are robbed at a restaurant or by a cook," said Lousteau.

Dinah makes the transformation from lady to housewife, and more is the pity. She loses all her charm in her lover's eyes. She would have done better to carry on eating out, even if that meant choosing a less expensive restaurant, for Paris was not short of good places to eat, less famous perhaps and less elegant, but still worth the detour.

Restaurants flourished so quickly and assumed such social importance after the Revolution that they could now be found all over the city. Balzac enjoyed walking around Paris; Gozlan describes endless walks with him, taken on the pretext of finding names for characters or ideas for novels by looking at signs and notices. One sign, depicting a clockface stopped at four o'clock, caught his eye. It was for a restaurant on the boulevard du Temple on the corner of the rue Charlot, far from the business center of the city, but that did not seem to matter. The food at the Cadran Bleu (Blue Clockface) was renowned, and attracted customers who enjoyed occasionally spending a bit of money to partake of it. The Cadran Bleu stuck to the tradition of a long table d'hôte in the middle of its main dining room, but had added some twenty individual tables and, more importantly, eighteen private dining rooms. It is a place where Vautrin, who knows it well, would be happy to bring the corpulent Madame Vauquer from the famous boardinghouse, to have mushrooms on toast. She would tighten her corset for these occasions, and put on an outfit that suggests another restaurant sign altogether . . . the one for the Boeuf à la Mode (the Fashionable Ox!). It is at the Cadran Bleu that the fearsome Madame Cibot, the evil concierge in *Cousin Pons*, becomes known as the Belle Ecaillère (the Beautiful Oyster Shucker). The boulevard du Temple specialized in rather saucy evening gatherings that went by a number of discreet euphemisms. A young man never went there alone.

Balzac traveled even farther, all the way to the Clichy toll-gate. Here, a cabaret that dated back to before the Revolution became famous in 1814 when it acted as headquarters for the Maréchal Moncey, who was resisting the Russians. With the return of the Bourbon kings, society figures flocked there to mingle with the common people and deal with rude waiters. The food was delectable, and Balzac offers as proof of this the loyalty displayed by the beggar of Saint-Sulpice, who, like any beggar who knows his job well, had amassed a fortune. Another place Parisians liked to go to be insulted was Katcomb, a peculiar establishment run by an Englishman on the ground floor of a building, when most restaurants were on the second floor. He served nothing but roast beef surrounded by potatoes, turnips, carrots, and beans. The tablecloths were changed only once a day, but each table had a brush with which customers could clear away crumbs. Every table also had a small carafe of wine. The prices were the same for everyone. So it comes as no surprise that Balzac sends a lowly clerk to eat there every day for twenty sous. Twenty sous, that is the sum each customer puts on the counter on the way out, and no one tips the serving girl, who, incidentally, treats everyone equally badly. It has to be said that the owner is far from amiable and tolerates neither recriminations nor requests.

There is also the Veau-qui-Tête (Suckling Calf) on the place du Châtelet, a meeting place for modest administrators and lovers of sheep's-foot dishes. Particular mention should be made of the Cheval Rouge (Red Horse), which was such a mediocre, unattractive place that people essentially went there when they did not want to be seen or heard by indiscreet observers. This was never easy. In a restaurant there was always a risk of being recognized or overheard even if you talked quietly in a private dining room. When Cerizet and Théodore, accomplices in foul play in *The Lesser Bourgeoisie*, have something to discuss, they think long and hard before opting for the Cheval Rouge on the quai de la Tournelle; there they can be sure they will meet no one at seven o'clock in the evening. Balzac knew the place well.

At one point Balzac had the idea of setting up a secret society for journalists, hoping this would garner him favorable reviews, but, in order to achieve this, the group had to meet somewhere discreet. His friend Gozlan described how the conspirators met at the Jardin des Plantes at four o'clock and set off together to eat in a restaurant that Balzac had discovered not far from there. The group followed him and, with a relaxed air, he stopped on the quai aux Vins beside the Tournelle Bridge. "Where we stopped," said Gozlan, "I could not see the least sign of a restaurant, or the suggestion of a café, but there was something unobtrusive, a crossbred looking place like a wine merchant's premises on the outskirts of the city. I looked up . . . and saw only a shapeless sign, hanging on the second floor of a narrow house. On the sign . . . I made out a huge rearing horse, painted in red . . . and written beneath its hooves were the words: *Au Cheval Rouge*! . . . The salon—it was really just a large space—that we stepped into perfectly matched the vulgarity of the sign; it was a warehouse at the far end of a courtyard, between a well and a shop selling empty casks . . . the red horses did not eat terribly well that first day."

With the Cheval Rouge we are venturing into the decidedly star-free territory of restaurants for students, places where a meal could be had for less than two francs. When these establishments sprang up, offering bourgeois amenities—choice on the menu and a clean table—for a modest price, even the notoriously thrifty Cousin Betty considered eating in a restaurant to be a reasonable choice for a bachelor. According to Brillat-Savarin, a good many restaurateurs realized that a substantial customer base of minor bourgeoisie, students, soldiers, clerks, and foreigners justified the effort of offering good cheap food. All they had to do was make palatable dishes using more beef than veal, more offal than cutlets, more herring, mackerel, whiting, or skate than sole and pike, poultry rather than game, and never any asparagus or strawberries but plenty of carrots, turnips, and potatoes. Most of these places were perfectly acceptable, although Lucien fumes at being reduced to eating for forty sous at Hurbain in Palais-Royal. Balzac also mentions Tabar, behind the rue Saint-Honoré, often used by the journalist Finot in his early days when he walked "on the uppers of his boots . . . His clothes hung together by some miracle as mysterious as the Immaculate Conception." Of all restaurants in this category, Flicoteaux, a large establishment in the Latin Quarter, is the one described in most detail. As I said earlier, Balzac used restaurants to move his plots forward: Flicoteaux and the Vauquer boardinghouse are the best examples of this.

The front door of Flicoteaux was on the place de la Sorbonne on the corner of the rue Neuve de Richelieu (which disappeared when the boulevard Saint-Michel was created). The constant stream of students passing before its windows saw not stuffed pheasants but large bowls of stewed plums and six-pound loaves of bread. The owner did not offer any sort of fantasy and was not interested in providing treats for the eye in favor of the stomach. There was a monastic simplicity to the two long dining rooms set at right angles. Its regulars and most numerous customers were young men who paid by the month; they each had a "table napkin slipped through a numbered shiny metal ring" that was set at their usual place. In the early days, the tablecloths were changed only on Sundays, but competition later forced Flicoteaux to change them twice a week. As Lucien observes: "There a dinner of three courses, with a quarter-bottle of wine or a bottle of beer, could be had for eighteen *sous*; or for twenty-two *sous* the quarter-bottle became a bottle. Flicoteaux, that friend of youth, would beyond a doubt have amassed a colossal fortune but for a line on his bill of fare, a line which rival establishments are wont to print in capital letters, thus—BREAD AT DISCRETION, which, being interpreted, should read 'indiscretion.' Flicoteaux has been nursing-father to many an illustrious name." The young eat quickly and the waiters, rather too few of them for the work, were prompt in serving a menu that offered no surprises.

The fare is not very varied. The potato is a permanent institution; there might not be a single tuber left in Ireland, and prevailing dearth elsewhere, but you would still find potatoes at Flicoteaux's. Not once in thirty years shall you miss its pale gold (the color beloved of Titian), sprinkled with chopped verdure; the potato enjoys a privilege that women might envy; such as you see it in 1814, so shall you find it in 1840. Mutton cutlets and fillet of beef at Flicoteaux's represent grouse and fillet of sturgeon at Very's; they are not on the regular bill of fare, that is, and must be ordered beforehand. Beef of the feminine gender there prevails; the young of the bovine species appears in all kinds of ingenious disguises. When the whiting and mackerel abound on our shores, they are likewise seen in large numbers at Flicoteaux's; his whole establishment, indeed, is directly affected by the caprices of the season and vicissitudes of French agriculture. By eating your dinners at Flicoteaux's you learn a host of things of which the wealthy, the idle, and folk indifferent to the phases of nature have no suspicion, and the student penned up in the Latin Quarter is kept accurately informed of the state of the weather and good or bad seasons. He knows when it is a good year for peas or French beans, and the kind of salad stuff that is plentiful; when [Les Halles] is glutted with cabbages, he is at once aware of the fact, and the failure of the beet crop is brought home to his mind. A slander, old in circulation in Lucien's time, connected the appearance of beefsteaks with a mortality among horseflesh.

Balzac pursued his long digression about Flicoteaux with observations on the clientele: unlike other restaurants mentioned, people did not go to Flicoteaux for fun or to watch other customers, and the novelist saw it as an opportunity to depict the new romantic generation:

Few Parisian restaurants are so well worth seeing. Everyone at Flicoteaux's is young; you see nothing but youth; and although earnest faces and grave, gloomy, anxious faces are not lacking, you see hope and confidence and poverty gaily endured. Dress, as a rule, is careless, and regular comers in decent clothes are marked exceptions. Everybody knows at once that something extraordinary is afoot; a mistress to visit, a theatre party, or some excursion into higher spheres . . . But with the exception of a few knots of young fellows from the same part of France who make a group about the end of a table, the gravity of the diners is hardly relaxed. Perhaps this gravity is due to the catholicity of the wine, which checks good fellowship of any kind. Those who frequented Flicoteaux's may recollect certain sombre and mysterious figures enveloped in the gloom of the chilliest penury; these beings would dine there daily for a couple of years and then vanish, and the most inquisitive regular comer could throw no light on the disappearance of such goblins of Paris. Friendships struck up over Flicoteaux's dinners were sealed in neighboring cafes in the flames of heady punch, or by the generous warmth of a small cup of black coffee glorified by a dash of something hotter and stronger.

Balzac makes these ironic remarks but concedes that the poorest provincial students found luxury at Flicoteaux's in comparison to the average family home, bringing them into line with Vautrin, who shudders as he imagines the chestnut soup that the poor Rastignacs feed off in the depths of the country.

Having said that, it should be pointed out that Balzac sends few students to Flicoteaux. The establishment is more like a club for struggling writers and journalists than a university canteen. The little group in *Lost Illusions* all meet there. There is no shame in that: Flicoteaux is not sinister in any way. It is here that we might find Lucien when, abandoned by his mentor, he has only two hundred francs left, has moved into a shabby hotel on the rue de Cluny very close to the Sorbonne, and eats here every evening. It is certainly worth arriving early in order to make the most of the choices on offer, as Lucien quickly discovers by sitting down to eat at about four o'clock. He wisely chooses a small table for two, near the counter, so that he can get to know the owner, which might prove useful in times of financial distress, and where he is intrigued by the pale handsome young man sitting facing him. After a week they start talking to each other, and Lucien learns from the woman on the counter that his new friend, Étienne Lousteau, is a literary and theater critic for an obscure newspaper. Lousteau vanishes as soon as he has any funds, and Lucien forbids himself the expense it would cost to follow him. Still at Flicoteaux's, he approaches Daniel d'Arthez, a young man of austere genius—as evidenced by the carafe of filtered water on his table—whose friends, including Bianchon, Bridau, and Michel Chrestien, are distinguished as much by their talent as their moral fiber. From this point on, Flicoteaux is depicted less as a restaurant than as a stage on which Lucien moves from one group to another, eventually betraying d'Arthez.

Truly needy students cannot afford Flicoteaux. They are to be found in the quarter's more dismal eating houses, which have leftovers all over the tables at the end of the evening, waiters sleeping in corners, "and a smell of cooking, lamp oil and tobacco [fills] the deserted room." Otherwise they might be in boardinghouses in the east end of the rue Saint-Jacques, closer to the Panthéon than to the Sorbonne, "a place where the sound of wheels creates a sensation; there is a grim look about the houses, a suggestion of a jail about those high garden walls . . . a suburb apparently composed of lodging-houses, . . . poverty and dullness." This is where we find the Vauquer boardinghouse, where the principal characters in *Father Goriot* congregate.

We need only imagine Madame Vauquer's dining room and the sort of food she offers her lodgers to start dreaming of Flicoteaux's. She sits eighteen lodgers around her long table, each paying thirty francs a month. Extras come at a price: fifteen francs a month for a shot of eau-de-vie in their coffee. Pickles and anchovies are reserved for the more generous lodgers. Not only is there no tablecloth, but the napkins—however stained they may be by food and wine—have to last a week, and the sideboards from which meals are served are sticky with dropped food. The most common dish is *haricot* mutton, one of Madame Vauquer's favorites (already mentioned by Molière's Harpagon), comprising a few cheap cuts that have been *haricotés* (boned), accompanied by carrots and turnips; it is one of the cheapest dishes in every working-class cook's repertoire. The leftovers are always reworked for the following day, served up with potatoes. The pears she serves are the least expensive available and are usually rotten, her black currant liqueur causes colic, and her biscuits are laced with mold. The only surprising detail: the cellar includes, as well as the everyday, some Laffitte and some champagne for which Madame Vauquer charges twelve francs, and she is always careful to combine what is left in the bottles

Madame Vauquer's dining room.

to make up a full one. The main differences here compared to the most modest restaurants are the enforced promiscuity and the total absence of intelligent conversation. The terrible, rowdy cacophony around the table constitutes the real horror of a boardinghouse. Rastignac escapes the place one day to go and visit his elegant cousin, the Vicomtesse de Beauséant, who invites him to stay for lunch, but he has to go home for dinner, and the contrast is unbearable:

Arrived in the Rue Neuve-Sainte-Genevieve, he rushed up to his room for ten francs wherewith to satisfy the demands of the cabman, and went in to dinner. He glanced round the squalid room, saw the eighteen poverty-stricken lodgers about to feed like cattle in their stalls, and the sight filled him with loathing. The transition was too sudden, and the contrast was so violent that it could not but act as a powerful stimulant; his ambition developed and grew beyond all bounds. On the one hand, he beheld a vision of social life in its most charming and refined forms, of quick-pulsed youth, of fair, impassioned faces invested with all the charm of poetry, framed in a marvellous setting of luxury or art; and, on the other hand, he saw a sombre picture, the miry verge beyond these faces, in which passion was extinct and nothing was left of the drama but the cords and pulleys and bare mechanism.

Paris offered this broad spectrum, but what of the rest of the country? Choice there was brutally restricted. Outside Paris there were no restaurants in the modern sense of the word. Even on the outskirts of the capital, at Saint-Cloud, it was impossible to have a *déjeuner*, a proper one with an appetizer, roast meat, poultry, and dessert. One day when Balzac and Gozlan were visiting the area, they had a sudden craving for food and stopped at an inn. They were served with mutton cutlets and a golden mountain of smelts. But they were still hungry. Sadly, no leg of lamb, no chicken fricassee, no veal fricandeau. "And do you have any sphinx?" Gozlan asked the astonished waiter, who went down to the kitchen to inquire. "Sphinx? Did you really ask for sphinx?" Balzac asked his companion. "Well, yes," he replied, "if you want a Paris *déjeuner* in a Saint-Cloud eatery, you might as well ask for a sphinx." The waiter came back up and announced that he was sorry but there was no sphinx left.

In the provinces, travelers were reduced to trusting to innkeepers, "all stereotyped by novel writers from the immortal Cervantes to the immortal Walter Scott. Are they not all boastful of their cookery? Have they not all 'whatever you please to order'? And do not all end by giving you the same scrawny chicken, and vegetables cooked with rank butter? They all boast of their fine wines, and all make you drink the wine of the country." They always run the best inn in their small town because they run the only one. Even the Burgundy drinking stall, the I Vert run by Madame Tonsard—a good cook, as it happens—in *Peasantry*, serves only overly spiced dishes in order to make its customers drink more. To eat well in the provinces a private invitation was needed. This was the case throughout the century, and only a country pharmacist like Homais in *Madame Bovary* can, in his naïveté, believe that the drowsy lobsters in a marble basin at the Café Normandie in Rouen promise any gastronomic delight.

Balzac had a passion for restaurants but knew full well that true luxury and exquisite refinement were not displayed in public places.

III

GREAT OCCASIONS

*B*alzac was both a realist novelist and an escapist dreamer, and nothing excited his imagination like a description of a meal. He documented, informed, and specified; then, weary of painting in detail, he transported himself to a magical world, in this instance the home of Taillefer the banker, a rather disturbing character with a vulgar, ruddy face. No one knows about Taillefer's criminal past, which is revealed in *The Red Inn*. His circumstances in Paris, sketched in *Father Goriot*, in which he appears as the young Victorine's very wealthy, grudge-bearing father, permit him to lay out the equally sumptuous and scandalous banquets described in *The Magic Skin*. Taillefer lives on the rue Joubert, in the newly fashionable Chaussée d'Antin neighborhood, and has summoned a number of successful Parisians—journalists, painters, poets, and politicians—to a reception intended to surpass "the circumscribed saturnalias of the petty modern Lucullus," as he promises his guests. His house takes luxury to extremes, and Balzac certainly enjoyed establishing the setting for the evening's festivities: "The rooms were adorned with silk and gold. Countless wax tapers set in handsome candelabra lit up the slightest details of gilded friezes, the delicate bronze sculpture, and the splendid colors of the furniture. The sweet scent of rare flowers, set in stands tastefully made of bamboo, filled the air. Everything, even the curtains, was pervaded by elegance without pretension, and there was a certain imaginative charm about it all which acted like a spell on the mind of a needy man."

A huge table welcomes the guests: "each paid his tribute of admiration to the splendid general effect of the long table, white as a bank of freshly-fallen snow, with its symmetrical line of covers, crowned with their pale golden rolls of bread. Rainbow colors gleamed in the starry rays of light reflected by the glass; the lights of the tapers crossed and re-crossed each other indefinitely; the dishes covered with their silver domes whetted both appetite and curiosity." The whiteness of the tablecloth is the first, indispensable sign of elegance. Its length is another: it was the height of luxury to have a tablecloth falling in large folds around the table legs. Balzac always mentions the state, quality, and whiteness of table linen when describing a meal, whether it be in a provincial town where, in order to honor a guest, "the damask linen marked 'A, B, C' was drawn from depths where it lay under a triple guard of wrappings, still further defended by formidable lines of pins"; out in the country where a refined cook would put thyme into the water when washing her linen to make the tablecloth scented; or in Paris, where a loving woman prepares an exquisite meal for two served on "a damask cloth that is dazzlingly white."

If care bestowed on table linen represented attention to detail in the setting, then the presence of silver domes on the table indicated munificence. All the dishes were laid out on the table, which meant the service would be conducted in the old-fashioned way, the French way, a spectacular form of service that required a great many servants. The dishes were arranged symmetrically on the table in keeping with a very precise and complicated plan, because poultry, roast meats, fish, shellfish, and vegetables were all presented simultaneously. No one expected it all to be eaten (hence the thriving leftovers market in Paris). If the butler did his job well, the visual impact was dramatic. He had to know how to use contrasting colors to best effect, to ensure that smaller game birds were reconstituted (a naked pheasant would

Two towering sugar constructions.

look meager), that roasts were surrounded by stuffing garnishes, and fish couched on a bed of greenery made from asparagus or spinach mousse. In the country, a feast might have been essentially a great accumulation of meat and poultry, but a gala meal in Paris was an opportunity to present a great variety of dishes where meat and fish, fruits and vegetables, ice creams and desserts had to be combined in a symphony of tastes and colors, often completely metamorphosing the ingredients. The plinths supporting stuffed turkeys and chickens were works of architecture, made of a mixture of lard and the fat from sheep's kidneys. They were sculpted to look like birds or fish, ornamented with pillars or machicolations, and decorated with griffins; it was often difficult to distinguish between the food itself and the structure displaying it. Originality in the presentation was as important as taste, which means the temperature of the room gave constant cause for concern: too cold and sauces would solidify, too hot and the plinths and complicated, towering desserts might melt and collapse. These desserts—the *extraordinaires,* to use Chef Carême's term—were incredible constructions in which threads of caramelized sugar were used to hold together profiteroles or meringues filled with cream, the only edible part of the concoction.

The meal had to look as beautiful as a painting, a sublime still life, but the gastronomic rewards did not always measure up to the presentation, because guests depended on a servant to put the dishes they had chosen onto their plates. Imagine how difficult it was to have something from a dish at the far end of the table if you did not have a valet constantly hovering at your elbow; think of the endless to and fro, and the irritation of not being able to taste every dish or simply the one dish you longed for, and add to this the disadvantage of eating it all cold. This whole performance was therefore costly, slow, and very frustrating if it was not carried out to perfection. Taillefer proves his love of excess and elaborate set dressing by refusing to give in to the new fashion known as Russian service (which is still used today), whereby servants present dishes—many fewer of them, of course—on the left-hand side of each guest. Carême very much liked Russian service, first introduced in Paris when the alliance was reached between Napoleon and the tsar, precisely because it brought the quality of the cooking more to the fore. For a number of years he recommended a mixed style of service where large joints of meat were displayed on the table but went untouched. Others were prepared specifically to be cut up and served to guests individually.

Under the July Monarchy, Russian service had not yet spread to the provinces. When Emma Bovary is invited to a grand dinner by the Marquis d'Andervilliers, it is not the gleaming silver domes positioned all the way down the table that astonish her, nor the juxtaposition of red-clawed lobsters, quails with all their feathers, roasted joints surrounded by truffles, and baskets lined with moss displaying layer upon layer of fruit, but the fact that the ladies did not put their gloves in their glasses. The marquis is so attached to old customs that for a gathering on this scale, he puts the men at a table in the hall and the ladies in the dining room, where he and the marquise preside.

The elaborate French style of service was progressively abandoned and remained a hallmark of great houses right up until the end of the Second Empire. In Émile Zola's *The Kill*, the fabulously wealthy Saccard gives a lavish dinner to impress potential associates. His butler recruits extra staff and creates a short-lived masterpiece: a table decorated with a vase at each end and lit by two ten-branched candelabra, between which there is a symmetrical line of warming stoves laden with sauces and main course dishes, as well as seashells containing the hors d'oeuvres. The centerpiece is so highly polished it creates a fountain of dancing candle flames. The success of a seated dinner like this, organized to proclaim the host's wealth and power, depended first and foremost on the pomp of the decor.

In fact Balzac was so convinced that show and splendor were the essential elements of a gala meal that he forgets to tell us what was actually eaten at Taillefer's feast, except to state that the menu would have been a credit to the late Cambacérès, and that Brillat-Savarin, the century's highest authority on gastronomy, would have applauded it. He may not discuss the solids at length, but the liquids are given his full attention. The formidable Taillefer wants to get his guests drunk, and he succeeds. Not only are the wines served in "royal profusion," but there is such a rapid succession of Madeira, Bordeaux, Burgundy, the "terrible" Rhône wines, and heady Roussillons that no one resists the combination: "Everyone ate as he spoke, spoke while he ate, and drank without heeding the quantity of the liquor, the wine was so biting, the bouquet so fragrant, the example around so infectious." The service is so quick and efficient that the guests have not a moment to stop and think until the time comes for the dessert to be served, and this requires a complete change of display, given that even the tablecloth disappears. Here again, Taillefer favors old customs, treating the meal like a stage play.

Between acts, the stage is empty for a moment; and between courses the table is stripped bare so that the valets can decorate it with large pieces of silverware, porcelain, or cut glass to create a new decorative theme. Taillefer opts for a huge gilded bronze tray from the workshops of Thomire, the greatest engraver and gilder of the time, and on it "tall statuettes . . . sustained and carried pyramids of strawberries, pineapples, fresh dates, golden grapes, clear-skinned peaches, pomegranates, Chinese fruit; in short, all the surprises of luxury, miracles of confectionery, the most tempting dainties, and choicest delicacies. The coloring of this epicurean work of art was enhanced by the splendors of porcelain, by sparkling outlines of gold, by the chasing of the vases. Poussin's landscapes, copied on Sèvres ware, were crowned with graceful fringes of moss, green, translucent, and fragile as ocean weeds. The revenue of a German prince would not have defrayed the cost of this arrogant display. Silver and mother-of-pearl, gold and crystal, were lavished afresh in new forms." This beautiful presentation has little effect on the guests, whose senses are dulled by the smells and vapors wafting from dessert wines. They all talk at the same time but listen to no one, and rehash the same old jokes without worrying about anyone's response. Eventually, whipped up by the "fiery sparks" of champagne, "impatiently expected and lavishly poured out," they become destructive: "The pyramids of fruit were ransacked, voices grew thicker, the clamor increased. Words were no longer distinct, glasses flew in pieces, senseless peals of laughter broke out." It came to the point when "the valets smiled," an incontrovertible sign of their masters' abject state.

Drunkenness, excess, and immoderation kill any possibility of conversation, which, rather than the need for nourishment, should have been the reason for bringing together so many different talents. The debauchery continues but not in the dining room: the butlers are firm yet tactful in directing the guests to the salon. A dinner served correctly should not have lasted more than three hours even in instances, like Taillefer's, when the guests were drunk, because it was vital to clear the table quickly. Once stripped of the delicacies they housed within their pillars of sugar, the magnificent temples and châteaus decorating the table were not for consumption. They were fragile and had to be moved back to the pantry as quickly as possible and handled with great care, because, even in the wealthiest households, they were used again. At the end of the meal the butler became a stage manager looking after the sets for his play. In restaurants, meals went on longer because, conversely, the establishment could only gain from serving drinks for as long as possible, and because the table was not decorated with such spectacular pieces.

Taillefer's orgiastic dinner clearly has a magical dimension in keeping with the element of fantasy and fable in *The Magic Skin*. Balzac therefore allows himself to succumb to what fascinates him: all the ceremony and splendor of presentation rather than a description of the food. For once, he barely refers to the cost of the meal (merely mentioning in passing that the feast cost more than two thousand écus, or ten thousand francs), and says nothing of the effort it would have taken to lay the meal out, nor what it reveals about the host's personality. Taillefer is the great provider but we will never know why he gave this wonderful feast or who prepared it.

Let us leave dreams in favor of reality, and see how a gala dinner would look in 1820s Paris in a household where economizing was giving way to social vanity. Once they had made a fortune, countless tradesmen wanted to pass themselves off as notable figures. How well you ate was one way of establishing a rise in status. More modest town dwellers were now aware of being judged on their ability to receive guests in style. But how were they to try their hand at it when they were not only unaccustomed to it but had no stylish staff? It goes without saying that even a capable family cook would have no idea how to put together a grand dinner, even less a collation served after a ball. For whatever reason, perhaps because Balzac never saw a great chef at work, there is a notable absence of great culinary artists in his novels. He does of course mention Carême, the inevitable Carême, the culinary genius of the time who trained on the job working in kitchens for Talleyrand, the famous chef to the prince regent, the tsar, and James de Rothschild; but rather than bringing him to life, he cites him symbolically or uses him as a reference. We know that Carême prepared an evening meal for the banker Nucingen every Sunday but we are never invited to join him. In other places, whenever Balzac mentions the presence of a chef it is either to have him dismissed for flagrant and scandalous theft, as with Count Octave's chef in *Honorine* (he fiddled the books so outrageously he could afford to open a restaurant), or to do without his services in order to economize, as Pierre Graslin does in *The Village Rector*. In fact, Balzac's characters—and I mean the Parisians—do not always need a chef because they have Chevet. Chevet is part of every festive dinner and sophisticated supper. But who or what on earth was Chevet?

Chevet was not only a *traiteur* (a supplier of prepared meals) but also a large grocery and a workshop where the best cooks were trained. It was Chevet who recommended Dunant to Bonaparte when he was looking for a chef, and the great Carême studied at Chevet's. Balzac, who was a loyal customer, felt the establishment was like a renowned review of fine food, a library of it, because the most exotic products were to be found there and fruits were always in season. In the middle of winter, it could supply fresh dates, oranges, and grenadines brought by steamboat from Sétubal, to the south of Lisbon. Under the Restoration, Chevet became an indispensable institution for a luxurious lifestyle. He could manage anything: Alexandre Dumas wanted to serve his guests with an extraordinary fish (a thirty-pound salmon or fifty-pound sturgeon), but did not have enough money for this whim, and anyway had no idea where to get hold of it. Undeterred, he went out hunting, came back with three roe deer, and offered them in exchange for the gigantic fish from Chevet. Sale! Nothing was impossible for Chevet. It was a ministry in its own right, declared the *Nouvel Almanach des Gourmands*, complete with couriers and chargés d'affaire and ambassadors. Its store acted as a political thermometer. In times of crisis, Monsieur Chevet was almost privy to state secrets; at the time food was like lubricating oil, helping the political mechanism run smoothly. Yet Chevet had a difficult start.

Before the French Revolution, Germain Chevet was a horticulturalist in Bagnolet; he supplied Versailles with roses. He was arrested in 1793 at the height of the Revolutionary Terror and owed his life to the fact that he was responsible for seventeen children, but he was forced to dig up his roses in order to plant potatoes. He gained so little from his new circumstances that he decided to try his luck in Paris. Renting premises at Palais-Royal, he specialized in small pastries, both sweet and savory, that were very fashionable at the time, but he also maintained a constant supply of fruit. After the Terror, he offered a wider selection, acquiring pineapples grown in pots under glass, and striving always to be the first to stock strawberries, cherries, or pears; eventually he came up with the idea of supplying lobsters, the largest oysters, and ready-prepared meals, whose inimitable smells drew customers to his store. Under the Empire, he became Talleyrand's supplier, and with that his fortune and reputation were made. When peace returned to Russia in 1815, the tsar called on him for major celebrations, and Chevet had the means to send a whole brigade of chefs and valets to Saint Petersburg, laden with the finest wines and foods. (Interestingly, from a current gastronome's point of view, he brought back neither caviar nor smoked salmon, which were not appreciated until the following century, but the fashion for decorating tables with flowers came from Russia.) As we have seen, serving such impressive customers did not stop him from delivering a dinner for two in prison as a favor to Balzac.

The latter returned the favor by making him the incomparable purveyor for all celebratory occasions in *The Human Comedy*. Chevet was no snob: he served kings but also newly rich merchants such as Birotteau, who wants to make a splash on the social scene; the elderly and very wealthy silk trader Camusot, who so desperately wants to please his pretty mistress, the divine Coralie; or the millionaire Crevel, who hopes to impress his rivals. Regimes came and went, and Chevet survived, and it is to Chevet that Flaubert sends Arnoux to buy a large hamper for his mistress and a choice of grapes, pineapples, and "other edible curiosities" for his wife.

Balzac had no hesitation in introducing real people into his novels, and it seems no one complained, even when he emphasized their less flattering characteristics and invented situations to act as a background for them. For example, Louis XVIII is a strong presence in almost a dozen novels. In *The Lily of the Valley*, he furthers Félix de Vandenesse's career, and Balzac describes him pointedly, specifically referring to his disenchanted and "deflowering" nature. He gently makes fun of Victor Hugo, who always inscribed the same four verses when people asked him to write in their albums. When he needs a composer, he calls on Rossini or Chopin; if he has to have a painter, he wheels in Gros, who, although "not very giving," goes on to help Joseph Bridau in the early days in *The Black*

Sheep. Editors, doctors, and booksellers are all mentioned by name. And Chevet seems to have been very grateful for the publicity Balzac gave him.

Let us look now at how Chevet comes to César Birotteau's rescue, and what this help costs the latter. Birotteau is a perfumer who has made a fortune. He is married to a very beautiful woman blessed with an excellent nature, who knows how to react sensibly in all situations, and is calm and reasonable. They have one adorable daughter: he has everything to make him the happiest of men, but he has political and social ambitions. As deputy mayor for the Second Arrondissement of Paris, he is decorated with the Légion d'Honneur, and to celebrate this honor he plans to give a ball preceded by a dinner and followed by a supper. But in order to do this and to create a dining room—a spectacular, Louis XIV-style dining room with a clock from Boulle, sideboards inlaid with brass and tortoiseshell, and fabrics draped on the walls with gilded tacks—he is forced to extend his rooms by renting the floor above. We shall bypass the tribulations caused by the building work insisted on by his architect, and the expensive hindrances brought up by the owner, in order to concentrate on preparations for the evening.

Madame Birotteau has agreed grudgingly to her husband's social extravaganza, but the complications horrify her. Where to buy silverware, glasses, and plates? Where would she find people she could trust as waiters? Who would watch the door to ensure no clever interlopers crept in without invitations? Lastly, who would prepare food magnificent enough to satisfy all the smart people Birotteau was planning to invite? César spares her all these concerns, thanks to the "diplomatic treaty" that he and the illustrious Chevet have signed. Chevet undertakes to provide resplendent silverware, "which earned him as much as a plot of land in rent," as well as supplying the dinner, wines, and staff under the orders of a suitable-looking butler, "in control of their every act and move." It was not a treaty between equals. If a newly wealthy man wanted to shine, he had to submit to the authority of a specialist. The roles of master and employee were reversed. There is no discussion about the menu or the overall price. Chevet insists that the kitchen and downstairs dining room be handed over to him entirely, so that he can set up his headquarters, although the space is barely adequate for serving up a dinner for twenty at six o'clock and a magnificent cold supper at one o'clock the following morning. Birotteau has come to an arrangement with the Café de Foy for the fruit-flavored ices, served on silver platters in pretty cups, with enameled spoons. Tanrade, another prized establishment, is to supply refreshments. On the appointed day, Chevet's people well and truly take possession of the apartment and set to work.

"The guests were punctual. The ordinary tradesman's dinner party followed, abundant in good humor and merriment, and enlivened by the homely jokes that never fail to provoke laughter. Ample justice was done to the excellent dishes, and the wines were thoroughly appreciated. It was half-past nine before they went into the drawing-room for coffee, and cabs had already begun to arrive with impatient dancers. An hour later, the rooms were full, and the dance had become a crush." Birotteau's guests have too much fun to keep hold of their newly acquired manners, and when the dance grows noisy the few aristocratic guests slip away, frightened off by the blazing lights and the exuberant abandon of those dancing, who know that the next day they will be plunged back into "the morass of chill reality." Has Birotteau achieved his goal? No, for one costly dinner is not enough to erase the social difference between the lesser bourgeoisie and high society or even the world of officialdom. Manners and good behavior cannot be acquired without a lengthy apprenticeship. At least the three Birotteaus have fun and go to bed tired but happy. Their happiness is short-lived, though: the colossal bill is presented a week later, and the unfortunate Birotteau is overwhelmed by the sum he owes, which runs to several tens of thousands of francs. Estimates are never respected in Balzac's world. That is one rule that suffers no exceptions.

Another rule—which Flaubert, Maupassant, and Zola also respected—dictated that any substantial function held in a house "where the traditions of grandeur had not descended through many generations" should end in disarray. The grand reception held by Madame de Beauséant in *Father Goriot* is the scene of subtle cruelties, but people's manners are no less unctuous for that. It is hard to imagine a guest succeeding in raising the tone any higher, or that anyone should tell a joke provoked by an excess of wine. But real excesses are found in Taillefer's home, Saccard's, and, on a smaller scale, Birotteau's or even the Thuilliers's (the main characters in Balzac's *The Lesser Bourgeoisie*): the shocking ostentation, shameless waste, and different wines poured indiscriminately. Parties always end in pandemonium in houses where the valets have more style than the masters. The impassioned set dresser in Balzac (who never quite switches off) is horrified by the disintegration of the set, a set that is such an integral part of the pleasure of a meal. Leftover food always provokes a shipwrecked feeling in Balzac. He is distraught at the pitiful sight of a partly dismantled table of food. "The dessert was like a squadron after a battle: all the dishes were disabled, pillaged, damaged; several were wandering around the table in spite of

The end of the party.

the efforts of the mistress of the house to keep them in their place." But Balzac emphasizes the point that, more than anything else, it is drunkenness that causes these debacles.

> "You are surprised as you enter the room at the neatness of the table, dazzling by reason of its silver and crystal and linen damask. Life is here in full bloom; the young fellows are graceful to behold; they smile and talk in low, demure voices like so many brides;

everything around them looks girlish. Two hours later you might take the room for a battlefield after the fight: broken glasses, serviettes crumpled and torn to rags lie strewn about among the nauseous-looking remnants of food on the dishes. There is an uproar that stuns you, jesting toasts, a fire of witticisms and bad jokes; faces are empurpled, eyes inflamed and expressionless; unintentional confidences tell you the whole truth. Bottles are smashed, and songs trolled out in the height of a diabolical racket; men call each other out, hang on each other's necks, or fall to fisticuffs; the room is full of a horrid, close scent made up of a hundred odours, and noise enough for a hundred voices. No one has any notion of what he is eating or drinking or saying. Some are depressed, others babble; one will turn monomaniac, repeating the same word over and over again like a bell set jangling; another tries to keep the tumult within bounds; the steadiest will propose an orgie. If anyone in possession of his faculties should come in, he would think that he had interrupted a Bacchanalian rite."

Zola was equally shocked by guests' behavior, but put less emphasis on drunkenness than a sort of madness paradoxically produced by the abundance of food. In this he differs from Balzac. Plenty of newly made men had humble beginnings but, as I said above, Balzac concentrates on either geniuses (such as Bridau or Despleins) or misers (like Monsieur Grandet, Séchard senior, or Gobseck) who count the value of every sou. Neither of these types has it in their nature to succumb to frenzied consumption. Zola depicts men for whom the importance of bread and the constant threat of privation are anchored in their minds and have assumed tremendous significance. For them the world is divided into the Fat and the Thin, and in order to stay in the ranks of the Fat, they exercise a sort of instinctive violence. It is therefore not drunkenness but a quasi-bestial voracity—encouraged by an absence of restraint in their masters and in other guests—that explains the scandals that occur at the end of some parties. During the course of a large gathering graced with sumptuous buffets at Saccard's house, the supper disintegrates into a real fight. The gluttony displayed by these well-behaved characters is boundless; they block the women's access to the buffet so that they can "swoop down on the pastries and truffled fowl, brutally digging others in the ribs. It was sheer pillage . . . The prefect had his eye on a leg of lamb. At just the right moment he reached out his hand . . . and calmly claimed his prize, having already stuffed his pockets with rolls. The gentlemen . . . did not even remove their gloves but inserted slices of lamb into

A sumptuous presentation of lobsters.

bread rolls while keeping bottles tucked safely under their arms. And, standing up, they chatted with their mouths full, jutting out their jaws so that the juice would fall on the carpet rather than on their coats." Only the servants maintain a degree of dignity: there will be plenty for everyone, the butler says soberly to the furious flood of diners while the staff grows impatient, astonished by how demanding the guests can be, still not contented after emptying three hundred bottles of champagne in a very short time.

It seems that a profusion of food and alcohol broke the recently acquired veneer of courtesy in new men, hence the extraordinary prestige still enjoyed by the old nobility. A feast or gala dinner in Paris was often the scene of a certain social tension either among the guests or for the host. Very frequently, one of the two parties did not know how to behave appropriately; it was almost inevitable that some code would disintegrate.

This discrepancy was not seen in the country, where class structures were more stable and everyone knew their place. During the peasants' celebration at Madame de Mortsauf's house in *The Lily of the Valley*, grape harvesters cheerfully lean on their elbows the length of the wooden table while the landowner's children mingle with them, but everything proceeds in an orderly, good-humored way. Even a large country banquet, the one celebrating Emma Bovary's marriage, does not end in confusion, despite the constant flow of cider, the carafes full of eau-de-vie and the glasses filled to the brim with wine; despite the incredible length of the meal (lasting sixteen hours); and despite the nature of the occasion, which lends itself to bawdiness. Some fall asleep at the table, others venture into song and try their luck with a show of strength, but conventions are respected; come the evening, Rouault, the father of the bride, is quite capable of ensuring there is no impropriety.

With great occasions, it is the master's authority, taste, and ambition that the novelist explores. The mistress of the house moves center stage when celebrations give way to the everyday.

IV

FAMILY LIFE

*H*owever much people eat out in Balzac's Paris, they still have a home life, and a great deal of family life happens at mealtimes. If, as I have pointed out, restaurants facilitate meetings between characters for the novelist, a family dining room gives the author an opportunity for real psychological studies. The way Monsieur Grandet makes the sugar disappear from the table or Monsieur Hochon (another elderly miser, who features in *The Black Sheep*) cuts the bread illuminates their characters. Little Pauline, in *The Magic Skin*, pouncing like a cat on a china bowl full of milk immediately captures the heart, while Father Goriot sniffing at his piece of bread seems both ridiculous and a little repulsive. These traits are like deft brushstrokes. But for Balzac, meals, which constitute "the surest thermometer for gauging the income of a Parisian family," illuminate the whole mechanism of the domestic system. What do people eat at home? How do they honor their guests? How do they shop for food? Do they order prepared meals from a *traiteur* or get up at dawn to dash to the market stalls at Les Halles? There are as many answers as there are characters.

There will be no exceptional banquets here, nor instances of out-and-out destitution where a few walnuts and three leaves of lamb's lettuce pass for a meal, but the everyday middle-class fare which forms the backdrop to *The Human Comedy*. It is worth noting that even for the wealthiest financiers, this everyday fare remains modest, if only in its lack of variety; only limited ingredients were available before the advent of the railway improved facilities for transporting goods. James de Rothschild's book of day-to-day menus offers proof of this: the baron's children ate chicken every evening except on New Year's Day, when they were entitled to fillet steak, and a rare few other occasions when they were given whiting. When the parents ate alone, the perennial chicken appeared again. For large dinners, Carême (and later his successor) would produce a joint of beef three or four times a week, varying only the trimmings. This would be followed by game, and the fish dish would always be salmon, a very common fish at the time, or turbot. Veal and mutton rarely appeared on the menu. Ox tongue and calves' sweetbreads were often ground up but were infrequently used as a main dish. Calves' liver, which is now highly prized, was kept for the servants' quarters. It was not until the middle of the century, when coastal train lines were set up, that fish from the sea became accessible to Parisians. Previously, it was thought that fish would spoil if transported more than forty leagues (one hundred miles) from where it was caught. People said it dried out or lost its flavor. In *A Start in Life*, the coach driver is in such a hurry that he turns down lunch because he has undertaken to deliver a large fish in good condition. Thirty years later, in *A Sentimental Education*, Flaubert describes Maurice Arnoux, a Parisian trader, boasting of having a trout from Geneva.

The astonishing diversity of Taillefer's feast became, if not commonplace, at least more accessible after the transport revolution. Ingredients were then not only fresher but more varied. What had once been the preserve of the highest lords could now be found on an ordinary Parisian's plate. Game came from Scotland, oranges from Spain, wine from South Africa. From as early as the Restoration, even modest office workers built up astonishing reserves in their cellars and larders. And the tendency to excess did nothing but flourish during the course of the century—excess in quantities and in how extravagantly food was prepared. Cheese is a striking example: during the Restoration, Parisians might nibble on a piece of cheese, occasionally some Brie, while under the Second Empire entire shops were devoted to butter and cheese from Normandy, the Auvergne, Picardy, Switzerland, or still farther afield. Zola describes two old women ensconced in the bustle of Les Halles, gossiping away amidst the powerful smell of Camembert, Limbourg, Marolles, Pont l'Évêque, and Livarot cheeses, amongst the giant Cantals, Cheshires, Parmesans, and Roqueforts under glass domes, "veined with blue and yellow, as if afflicted by some shameful disease for rich people who have eaten too many truffles."

When he is invited to dinner at Arnoux's house, Frédéric, the hero of *A Sentimental Education,* "had to choose between ten mustards. He ate daspachio, curry, ginger, blackbirds from Corsica, lasagna from Rome." Arnoux, a porcelain manufacturer, is not in possession of a great fortune but prides himself on being a good host. He "cultivated all the mail coach drivers to secure foodstuffs, and had connections with cooks in grand houses, who gave him recipes for sauces." Like many Parisians, he has no hesitation in spending a great deal of money both at home and in restaurants. "The tyranny of the palate has never been described; as a necessity of life it escapes the criticism of literature; yet no one imagines how many have been ruined by the table. The luxury of the table is indeed, in a sense, the courtesan's one competitor in Paris," says Balzac in *Cousin Pons*.

One constant in this society was the presence of servants: however few or many of them there were and however well trained they may have been, they were always there. Even the most modest shopkeeper's household depended if not on a cook, at least on a housemaid. The only exceptions are the moneylender Gobseck, a pathologically secretive character who cannot abide any curiosity about his life, and Sylvie Rogron, who dismisses her cook in a frantic bid to save money, claiming that "she herself cooked 'to amuse herself.'" As a general rule, in Balzac's world the quality and appeal of a meal are as much the product of a servant's talent as her honesty and the relationship she has with her employers. These servants are inevitably women, because, as mentioned above, there are no active chefs in Balzac's work.

Let us return briefly to Madame Marneffe, the woman too preoccupied with other matters to attend to her household. Not only does her cook overcharge her for the food she buys, she also serves her uneatable roast joints because she has drained all the juices to dress up the leftovers she keeps for her boyfriend. On top of this, the woman neglects her chores, and "the dining-room, badly kept by the single servant, had the sickening aspect of a country-inn; everything looked greasy and unclean." A cut of veal swimming in reddish water masquerading as cooking juices constitutes the mainstay of the meal, and is "served and eaten in cracked plates and dishes with dull-looking and dull-sounding German silver . . . The dingy decanters could not disguise the vile hue of wine bought by the pint at the nearest wineshop. The table-napkins had seen a week's use. In short, everything betrayed undignified penury, and the equal indifference of husband and wife to the decencies of home." Indeed, the only ruse Madame Marneffe conceives to escape their straitened circumstances is to seduce a rich protector, Baron Hulot as it happens, something she does with her husband's complicity, and does so avidly that she reduces her benefactor to the most humiliating ruin. Readers quickly deduce that Madame Marneffe loves no one—a woman who knows how to love can learn to economize and "live in comfort on [a] narrow income." It does not take much to mask the ignominy of poverty, but only loving women know how. Lucien Rubempré's ambitions, for example, are supported by a trio of women: his sister Eve and his mistresses Coralie and Esther, all three of whom suffer for their affection. Balzac illustrates how sincere their love for him is by the care they put into feeding him. Despite her severe financial limitations, Eve knows the art of presenting something simple like strawberries on a pretty plate garnished with leaves, and Coralie, the young courtesan, is so hopelessly in love with him that even when she has fallen into destitution she manages to serve him a charming dinner of scrambled eggs. In *Eugénie Grandet*, Balzac has fun showing the reader how Eugénie starts to use her imagination and even to become inventive when she falls in love with her cousin. Despite her father's rigorous supervision, she succeeds in building a precarious pyramid of pears and grapes for the young man's lunch. Madame Marneffe is not the sort to busy her little white hands with that kind of thing, and is therefore utterly dependent on her maid.

There was inevitably a significant amount of theft among suppliers and staff, and this issue seems to have obsessed Balzac, unlike Zola, who put his emphasis on how cruelly servants were treated. The conservative Balzac felt that "in every household the plague of servants is nowadays the worst of financial afflictions," and he showed little indulgence for the servant who was effectively a "domestic robber, a thief taking wages, and perfectly barefaced." According to him, theft was so widespread in Paris that it required round-the-clock surveillance. Only the greatest misers and women who were very careful with their housekeeping money avoided this bloodletting. The fact that Madame Marneffe's household recovers is due to Lisbeth, also known as Betty, her lover's cousin, who takes things in hand. The first task Betty assigns herself is to dismiss the disgraceful maid, because she knows that the servants have set up a secret toll system between the market and their masters' table, even going so far as to persuade shopkeepers to increase their written receipts by 50 percent. The only way to run a household economically is to watch over the cook and teach her to do her buying in the market instead of going to suppliers who have no qualms about pumping up the bill. That is what the formidable Betty does when she reorganizes her friend Valérie's house. A relation of hers once worked for the bishop of Nancy, a telling detail because, according to Balzac, doctors and men of the cloth were great specialists in gastronomy. "So she had brought from the depths of the Vosges a humble relation on her mother's side, [this] very pious and honest soul . . . Fearing, however, her inexperience of Paris ways, and yet more the evil counsel which wrecks such fragile virtue, at first Lisbeth always went to market with Mathurine, and tried to teach her what to buy. To know the real prices of things and command the salesman's respect; to purchase delicacies [unaffected by the seasons], such as fish, only when they were cheap; to be well informed as to the price current of groceries and provisions, so as to buy when prices are low in anticipation of a rise,—all this housekeeping skill is in Paris essential to domestic economy. As Mathurine got good wages and many presents, she liked the house well enough to be glad to drive good bargains." Going to market guaranteed the best price but also the best quality, and this was true right up until the twentieth century. Proust's narrator (probably persuaded by his mother) sends the family cook there to buy the necessary ingredients to make her beef en gelée a masterpiece.

But going to the central market was no mean feat. When Balzac was planning to hire a cook whom his sister had to let go for financial reasons, he made it a condition that she agreed to buy from Les Halles as restaurateurs and fruit sellers did. She refused, because it took exceptional energy to get up at dawn and barter with the vendors. When money was very tight, he was therefore reduced to hiring a woman who came in on Mondays to prepare meals for the entire week—despite his horror of cold meat. When he reached the end of his beef or mutton dish, he had to make do with bread, cheese, and potatoes like the Irish.

The marketplace of Les Halles was in fact a building site at the time. In 1811 Napoleon had started a project to replace the old wooden hangars and their stalls, open to the four winds, with a modern construction, but the work was not finished before the Second Empire. The regulars at Les Halles treated themselves to eau-de-vie spiked with pepper, and the overall

The bustling scene at Les Halles, the central market.

noise and commotion was hardly designed to attract the faint-hearted. Even an old Parisian like the perfumer Birotteau, when looking for the hazelnuts he needs for his hair oil, has trouble making his way through the labyrinth "of slums which are, as it were, the entrails of Paris. Here countless numbers of heterogeneous and nondescript industries are carried on; evil-smelling trades, and the manufacture of the daintiest finery, herrings and lawn, silk and honey, butter and tulle, jostle each other in its squalid precincts. Here are the headquarters of those multitudinous small trades which Paris no more suspects in its midst than a man surmises the functions performed by the pancreas in the human economy." Cousin Betty, who is afraid of nothing, is commendably successful: to Madame Marneffe's tremendous credit, her dinners bring together artists, politicians, and her lovers' friends.

Sadly, Cousin Pons and his friend Schmucke lack this attention to detail and knowledge of current prices when they try to keep an eye on their concierge, Madame Cibot, who cooks their meals and, in so doing, leads them to ruin. She boasts to her husband that she has amassed two thousand francs in eight years thanks to her cunning and talent. In fact, rather than going to a butcher, she rummages through the stalls at a *regrattier,* who buys leftovers from nearby restaurants. With a fiercely discerning eye, she chooses the best-looking debris of chicken or game, fish fillets, or even boiled beef, which she dresses up with finely sliced onion. Using this technique, she cooks such strong-smelling sauces that her lodgers never complain, and she makes them pay three francs "without wine" for these dinners, a sizable sum if we consider that, in a modest but acceptable restaurant, a meal with a small carafe of wine cost a maximum of two francs.

This sort of misadventure was not likely to happen to Madame Guillaume, the draper's wife in *At the Sign of the Cat and Racket.* She is so horrified at the thought of potential waste that not only does she trust no one else to pour oil over the salad, but she herself does it with such a sparing hand that she barely moistens the leaves. By way of dessert, she serves Gruyère—which was a poor man's cheese at the time—and Gruyère so old that her staff has fun carving the date on it. Less meticulous women were either ignorant of the full extent of the damage or resigned to being robbed by their cooks, and, in Paris, the cooks were cheekily aware of the fact. It is hardly surprising that it was essential for well-brought-up young ladies to learn—from watching their mothers—to scold the cook. Otherwise, they would soon find that a serving girl who "entered [their] service without effects, without clothes, and without talent, has come to get her wages in a blue merino gown, set off by an embroidered neckerchief, her ears embellished with a pair of ear-rings enriched with small pearls, her feet clothed in comfortable leather shoes which give you a glimpse of neat cotton stockings. She has two trunks full of property, and keeps an account at the savings bank."

Madame Guillaume is head of only a very small household constituting her husband, her two daughters, and her staff; Thuillier's family is more complex. Thanks to them, we venture into the day-to-day lives of minor Parisians striving to get somewhere in the world. They illustrate a rise in social standing which translates into a need to receive guests, but this rise has not given them time to train servants, and they are not sufficiently ambitious to contemplate taking on more.

We are in the Thuillier household, a ménage à trois, in the most honorable sense of the expression. It comprises Monsieur Thuillier, his wife, and his sister Brigitte, one of those formidable Balzacian old maids. Mademoiselle Thuillier makes quick work of crushing her sister-in-law, and reigns imperiously over her mediocre brother, a deputy chief clerk who resigns after 1830. She is the one who holds the purse strings and she holds them very tightly, because the purse has been as good as empty for a long time. These characters are the children of the first concierge to the Ministry of Finance (who managed to top up his salary by operating an unofficial canteen in his quarters, while instructing his daughter in the art of feeding customers for as little as possible), and they have certainly succeeded in life, but they had a difficult start and had to show great patience before attaining a respectable social position and any financial security.

The son, Jérôme, who was too shortsighted to be drafted, managed to exploit the fact that under the Empire the profusion of jobs within the army created a lack of personnel in minor civilian administrative roles. He therefore had no trouble climbing up the lower rungs of the bureaucratic hierarchy, and his ignorance taught him to keep his mouth closed—which made him an excellent employee. His sister chose work known only to those familiar with the Ministry of Finance: making the special bags that the Central Bank, the Treasury, and the major financial institutions used to transport notes and coins. Everyone at the ministry had known her since she was a child; her diligence was appreciated and she made rapid progress. In her third year she had two women working for her; she made a note of her savings in a ledger and, in 1814, found she had amassed 3600 francs in fifteen years. She spent little and ate with her father almost every evening while he was alive. When he died the brother and sister decided to pool their resources, increasing these further with revenue from a building that Brigitte had succeeded in buying. This arrangement was not undermined when Jérôme married.

The novel, set in 1839, depicts the modest and hardworking bourgeoisie who formed the basis for the July Monarchy. Thuillier's position in their small social circle has reached the  point where they receive friends twice a month and serve them an impressive dinner. What *was* an impressive dinner to the minor bourgeoisie? That is what Balzac—focusing this time on reality—takes great pleasure in describing.

Monsieur Thuillier warns his sister that there will be at least fifteen for dinner, but omits to inform her that the excellent news of his virtually guaranteed election to the town council will be announced over dessert. Brigitte therefore sets to work complaining about the cost, which, she calculates, will be no less than forty francs, unless she manages to use the leftovers to feed the family for the next two days. She has her servants lay out a magnificent tablecloth for the occasion and take out the elaborate old silverware, a treasure that Thuillier the elder bought during the Revolution and which served him well in the days when he ran the clandestine restaurant in his quarters. The setting would, therefore, be perfectly elegant were it not for two hideous silver-plated copper candlesticks, each with four branches bearing the most economical kind of candles made of beef lard. Habits learned in a household where every sou has been counted for many years die hard. And Balzac goes on to point out that when they see the table, one or two guests familiar with superior luxuries exchange discreet smiles "expressing a complicity of satirical thoughts." Naturally, the cooking bears witness to the parsimony exercised by the mistress of the house. It is clear to everyone that she is responsible for the whole evening—Balzac even tells us she is the very model of an 1840 bourgeois cook—and her two servants are not allowed to take any initiatives. The key to the wine cellar never leaves her belt.

The soup was a rather pale bouillon; for, even on an occasion like this, the cook had been enjoined to make a great deal of bouillon out of the beef supplied. Then, as the said beef was to feed the family on the next day and the day after that, the less juice it expended in the bouillon, the more substantial were the subsequent dinners. The beef, little cooked, was always taken away at the following speech from Brigitte, uttered as soon as Thuillier put his knife into it:—

"I think it is rather tough; send it away, Thuillier, nobody will eat it; we have other things."

The soup was, in fact, flanked by four viands mounted on old hot-water chafing-dishes, with the plating worn off. At this particular dinner (afterwards called that of the candidacy) the first course consisted of a pair of ducks with olives, opposite to which was a large pie with forcemeat balls, while a dish of eels "a la tartare" corresponded in like manner with a fricandeau on chicory. The second course had for its central dish a most dignified goose stuffed with chestnuts, a salad of vegetables garnished with rounds of beetroot opposite to custards in cups, while lower down a dish of turnips "au sucre" faced a timbale of macaroni.

In the Thuillier household we see the poor man's version of the old-style service that is depicted in all its splendor at Taillefer's feast. The table is not dressed up with any aesthetic considerations, apart from the cleanliness of the tablecloth. The food is fairly abundant; the macaroni adds a note of refinement, but the preponderance of poultry, the absence of game, and the dearth of vegetables demonstrate a concern to avoid waste. It is all perfectly decent, but there is a suspicion that nothing really tickles the guests' appetites, as nothing has been planned with their pleasure in mind. The meal is a scene of rowdy disorder because the young maid cannot possibly serve everyone single-handed. During this rather vulgar dinner, those in the know announce Jérôme's likely election; this causes an uproar, and Brigitte, forgetting her terror at the expense of entertaining, descends on her cook, bellowing at her to come down to the cellar with her and bring up some of the wine they keep for special occasions.

The sudden profusion of wines and liqueurs, and the delicacies produced from the depths of cupboards, prove the remarkable stores of alcohol and sweetmeats in an otherwise extremely modest household. Brigitte actually comes back with three bottles of champagne. We should not be too surprised that these lowly people have such an abundance of this festive wine. A liking for champagne developed late in France, much later than in England. Madame de Pompadour, one of the first ladies to appreciate it, launched the fashion for it. Its production, however, was still very limited, despite increasing demand under the Empire. This was partly due to the fact that the bottles often exploded in storage; a wine producer could lose 30 to 40 percent of his production in this way. It was only toward 1830 that champagne producers perfected a reliable technique for measuring the wine's sugar content, thereby avoiding such violent fermentation. Bottles could now tolerate the pressure, and production rose very rapidly, going from 300,000 bottles in 1785 to seven million in 1844; hence the reserves kept even by the most thrifty families. As well as the champagne, Brigitte produces three bottles of old Hermitage wine, three bottles of a good vintage of Bordeaux, a bottle of Malaga, and one of 1802 eau-de-vie that her father bought and that she carries with almost respectful care, using it to flavor the orange salad that she asks her sister-in-law to make on the spot.

This orange salad is merely a prelude to the dessert course, where the women pile the table high with heaps of mixed dried fruits (almonds, hazelnuts, figs, and raisins) and pyramids of apples, cheeses, jams, and crystallized fruit. Sudden happiness at the good news translates into this avalanche of sweet foods. The old maid also promises punch, *marrons glacés*, meringues, and, the height of extravagance, some tea that she sends for from the pharmacy, because tea was so rare that it was sold by the apothecary, as sugar once was.

What is striking in this description is how substantial this modest household's stores are and how good their wines. It could be that wine was accumulated as a secure asset, but what of their provisions of fruit compotes and conserves? Might they be a common precaution in a century so scarred by revolution and unrest? Be that as it may, delighted by this unhoped-for treat, the diners gorge themselves and get drunk. The only two connoisseurs among the guests are distressed by this universal gluttony: it is murder, one whispers in the other's ear, to give such good Malaga wine to such lowly palates. Brigitte, who, according to her sister-in-law, really works like a horse, keeps her composure amidst all the uproar and takes it into her head to get people dancing to end the evening. Rumors of a party at the Thuilliers' circulated among their friends around the Jardin du Luxembourg earlier in the day and attract a number of young people after the dinner, a liberty that gives the neighborhood an almost provincial tone.

Lending a hand to her two servants, [Brigitte] cleared the table, taking everything out of the dining-room to accommodate the dancers, vociferating, like the captain of a frigate on his quarter-deck when taking his ship into action.

"Have you plenty of raspberry syrup? Run out and buy some more orgeat!" or "There are not enough glasses. Where's the 'eau rougie'? Take those six bottles of 'vin ordinaire' and make more. Mind that Coffinet, the porter, doesn't get any! Caroline, my girl, you are to wait at the sideboard; you'll have tongue and ham to slice in case they still dance till morning. But mind, no waste! Keep an eye on everything. Pass me the broom; put more oil in those lamps; don't make blunders. Arrange the remains of the dessert so as to make a show on the sideboard!"

One of the guests, a musician in his time, gives the signal to dance

by tuning his clarionet, the joyous sounds of which were greeted with huzzas from the salon. It is useless to describe a ball of this kind. The toilets, faces, and conversations were all in keeping with one fact which will surely suffice even the dullest imagination; they passed round, on tarnished and discolored trays, common tumblers filled with wine, "eau rougie," and "eau sucrée." The trays on which were glasses of orgeat and glasses of syrup and water appeared only at long intervals. There were five card-tables and twenty-five players, and eighteen dancers of both sexes. At one o'clock in the morning, all present—Madame Thuillier, Mademoiselle Brigitte, Madame Phellion, even Phellion himself—were dragged into the vivacities of a country-dance, vulgarly called "La Boulangère," in which Dutocq figured with a veil over his head, after the manner of the Kabyl. The servants who were waiting to escort their masters home, and those of the household, were audience to this performance; and after the interminable dance had lasted one whole hour it was proposed to carry Brigitte in triumph when she gave the announcement that supper was served. This circumstance made her see the necessity of hiding a dozen bottles of old burgundy. In short, the company had amused themselves so well, the matrons as well as the young girls, that Thuillier found occasion to say:—

"Well, well, this morning we little thought we should have such a fete to-night."

"There's never more pleasure," said the notary Cardot, "than in just such improvised balls. Don't talk to me of parties where everybody stands on ceremony."

This opinion, we may remark, is a standing axiom among the bourgeoisie.

Brigitte's success derives not from the excellence of the meal she serves but from the spontaneity of her party. Of course, the profusion of wines and spirits brightens the gathering, and the Thuilliers' happiness is contagious, but the total absence of pretension has its part to play too. Unlike Birotteau's reception, Brigitte's is not calculated. She violates her usual thriftiness, not to achieve anything but to celebrate her brother's success, hence the pleasure with no ulterior motive.

In his Parisian novels, then, Balzac does not dwell much on how the meal is prepared or on the food itself. According to him, "in Paris people eat [half-heartedly] and trifle with their pleasure"; in society, people do not go out to enjoy a delicious meal but to do business, to conspire, to hear the latest news, and to make sure they are seen. Among successful Parisians, a pleasantly entertaining drawing room and excellent food are taken for granted; they go unnoticed and are never referred to. So, although Balzac mentions the talented Sophie, Comte Popinot's cook, whose "fat Rhine carp with a sauce, thin in the sauce-boat and creamy upon the palate," makes the peerless gastronome Cousin Pons swoon, he does not describe her. He never shows the women busying away over a hot stove except in the utterly exceptional case of the fateful Asie, Vautrin's aunt. She is an accomplice to his crimes and unequaled in her ability to "turn you out a simple dish of beans that will make you wonder whether the angels have not come down to add some herb from heaven," but is equally able to inject enough poison into the cherries in a tutti-frutti ice cream to kill the policeman, Peyrade, who had the audacity to challenge her nephew! We have to go out to the provinces to get inside people's kitchens.

*J*N THE provinces, the lack of occupation and the monotony of life lead the mind to expend its surplus energy upon the kitchen. People do not dine so luxuriously in the provinces as in Paris, but they dine better; the dishes are carefully considered and studied. In the heart of the provinces there are Carêmes in short petticoats, unknown unsung geniuses, who can make a simple dish of *haricots verts* worthy of the nod of the head with which Rossini greets anything that is perfectly successful." These cooks were not experts in clever sauces; they would not have found work in the new restaurants where the staff had to know a hundred different ways of preparing things; and they would have been shocked by the cunning used in masking tastes. In these honest women's eyes, Madame Cibot was a poisoner. Their talent lay in knowing how to use cheap, simple ingredients. It is worth pointing out that these are not peasants, but women with practical experience. Balzac had little affection for peasants. In a novel called *The Peasantry*, he describes in unflattering terms the kitchen run by La Tonsard, wife of a notorious poacher. This woman opens a refreshments stall, a very basic sort of café, to make a profit from the products of her husband's and sons' nocturnal expeditions, and she puts her talents into "dishes well known in the country, such as jugged hare, game, sauce, sea-pie, and omelettes, [and] she was supposed to understand to admiration the art of cooking a meal served at a table's end, and so prodigiously over-seasoned that it induces thirst."

On the other hand, in the same novel, he takes pleasure in lingering over every last gastronomic detail in relation to the modest but fearsome Grégoire Rigou, who is mayor of a village of some sixty houses. Balzac was interested in Rigou because this "miser full of tender cares for his own comfort" was representative of a kind of rural existence that was specific to France and in which "his fashion of blowing the fire, his habits at table, his opinions and way of life—none of these things are insignificant from this point of view."

Rigou was a monk who made the most of the Revolution to escape his Benedictine monastery and turn his hand to studying law. In 1815 he is not only mayor but also a state prosecutor, and he goes into moneylending with remarkable success. He marries the housekeeper of the late village priest. A former brother from the abbey clings to him like a dog and becomes groom, gardener, cowherd, personal valet, and steward to this sensual Scrooge who, Balzac is at pains to point out, eats and drinks like Louis XIV.

How does he live so well? First, he reduces his wife to total obedience and, as soon as she loses her bloom, he insists that she employ a pretty young serving girl, whom he replaces every three years. His policy is to hire girls at sixteen and send them away at nineteen. To fine-tune this arrangement, he sleeps in a separate bedroom, and his bed, where "the mattresses were of the best, the sheets fine and soft . . . [and] ample curtains shut out cold draughts," would have satisfied the most demanding Parisienne. On top of this, he eats alone, served by his wife, who eats after he has finished, in the kitchen with their two servants while he digests his meal and sleeps off his wine in peace, and what wine it is too! While Madame Rigou has to make do with local wine, he savors the finest Burgundies, and exquisite vintages from Bordeaux, Champagne, Roussillon, the Rhône, and Spain.

Dinner, breakfast, and supper alike were composed of dishes exquisitely prepared with the culinary skill in which a curé's housekeeper excels the rest of her sisterhood. Mme. Rigou herself, for instance, churned twice a week. Cream entered into every sauce. Vegetables, gathered at the last moment, were transferred as it were straight from the garden into the pot. Parisians are so accustomed to garden stuff which has lain sweltering in a shop exposed to the genial influences of the sun, the tainted air of city streets, and the green-grocer's watering can, all promotive of a specious freshness, that they have no idea of the delicate, fugitive flavours of vegetable products when eaten in some sort "alive."

The Soulanges butcher supplied his best meat, under penalty of losing the redoutable Rigou's custom. The poultry were reared at the house, to ensure superlative excellence.

Madame Rigou's cooking represents Balzac's gastronomic ideal: fresh ingredients with no added spices whatsoever, allowing the natural flavor (so impossible to have in Paris) to triumph. Ironically, he bestows its benefits on Rigou, whose "exaggeratedly wide mouth and thin lips betrayed their owner for an undaunted trencherman, and a valiant drinker by a certain droop at the corners, where two comma-shaped slits slobbered perpetually while he ate or talked." But food lovers, as we shall see, are rarely sympathetic characters in Balzac's work, and there is not a single character to be found who is both virtuous and preoccupied with his or her stomach; hence the marked difference between Rigou and the country doctor, Dr. Bénassis, one of *The Human Comedy*'s saints, one of those saints whose painful and perhaps guilty past catches the reader's attention.

The doctor lives alone in the country, and without his wonderful Jacquotte he would lead an ascetic life. This Jacquotte who watches over him is the most endearing of Balzac's servants, the sort of woman most people would love to see looking after a son or a bachelor uncle. And Bénassis certainly needs her, because this simple, generous man, immune to the material things around him, lives only to do good to others. Like so many good cooks, Jacquotte was also trained by a priest, an ecclesiastical gourmet whose vegetable garden enjoyed local renown. When Bénassis moves into the area, he buys the late priest's house along with its entire contents, furniture, crockery, linen, wine cellar, chickens, carriage, and horse. And he asks the valet and cook to stay in his service. Jacquotte, who "was the very pattern of a working housekeeper, with her clumsy figure, and her bodice, always of the same dark brown print with large red spots on it, which fitted her so tightly that it looked as if the material must give way if she moved at all," takes control of the household. Her master never interferes nor makes the slightest comment to her. He asks for only two things: to have dinner at six o'clock and to spend no more than a certain amount every month. Jacquotte is perfectly happy with this arrangement. She establishes the menus, oversees the valet and the stable, stores up provisions, and decides when the pigs should be slaughtered. Neither the master nor the valet risks questioning her decisions, in order to avoid lengthy remonstrance. "A woman whom every one obeys in this way is always singing, so Jacquotte laughed and warbled on the staircase; she was always humming something when she was not singing, and singing when she was not humming." She would tell anyone who cared to listen that if he had to live without her, "it would have been a sad thing for M. Bénassis . . . for the poor man was so little particular that you might feed him on cabbage for partridges, and he would not find it out."

She gives the vegetable garden her wholehearted attention, because she is determined to maintain the tradition insisted on by the priest, whose spirit still seems to inhabit the house. A good vegetable garden supplied fruits and vegetables all year round. Balzac, a passionate lover of pears, must have known that Louis XIV's horticulturalist, La Quintinie, succeeded in introducing forty-six varieties of pear: nine for the summer, ten for the autumn, and twenty-seven for the winter. Jacquotte cannot lay claim to such profusion, but good native of the Savoie region that she is, there is no doubting she prides herself on her winter cabbages and her Italian summer cabbages. She also has to ensure that the garden's protective walls are in a fit state and to take care of watering. Thanks to her efforts, the doctor and his staff live almost self-sufficiently. The doctor may well be indifferent to things around him, but it is the indifference of a man who is prey to an obsession (he has ambitions to transform the local economy). Jacquotte completely accepts his detachment, even proving rather irritable when he inquires about a room he is planning to give to a guest. Not only is the room perfect, with the bed made up as if for a new bride, but Jacquotte also takes the newcomer a glass of milk at bedtime. She thinks of the house as her own. From the very first meal described in the novel, we feel we are in good hands.

On days when a distinguished guest warrants a degree of ceremony, the table is covered with a cloth of that "peculiar kind of damask linen invented in the time of Henry IV by the brothers Graindorge, the skilful weavers, who gave their name to the heavy fabric so well known to housekeepers. The linen was of dazzling whiteness, and fragrant with the scent of the thyme that Jacquotte always put into her wash-tubs. The dinner service was of white porcelain, edged with blue, and was in perfect order. The decanters were of the old-fashioned octagonal kind still in use in the provinces, though they have disappeared elsewhere. Grotesque figures had been carved on the horn handles of the knives. These relics of ancient splendor, which, nevertheless, looked almost new, seemed to those who scrutinized them to be in keeping with the kindly and open-hearted nature of the master of the house."

The stock is the most substantial any cook ever simmered and reduced. Now, this is something on which Balzac was categorical: if the stock was good, the household was to be trusted. There is no doubting that Jacquotte makes it the old-fashioned way, adding very little water to the meat and letting it simmer for hours on end, repeatedly removing any scum. When it has finished cooking, she strains it through muslin. Using this method, she makes clear stock thickened only by the gelatin extracted from the bones. This utterly simple perfection, obtained through the cook's patience, characterizes everything that is good about the provinces. Balzac was so interested in stock that he did not abandon the subject before mentioning a different type that Jacquotte prepares, snail stock, which has such invigorating qualities that the doctor takes some to his patients. This remedy was so frequently used at the time that Carême provided a recipe for it: take twelve snails and four dozen frogs' legs, and poach them in water with leeks and small turnips. Strain the stock, color it with saffron, and drink it morning and evening.

The only criticism Balzac would level at this domestic goddess is that she serves dinner by bringing the dishes in one at a time, a custom that Balzac loathed because it had the disadvantage of making greedy people eat excessively and making more sober eaters neglect the best food because their hunger was sated with the very first dish. Jacquotte's only regret is that she is rarely complimented: this is because food is not the high point of the doctor's day; he sits down to a meal not for entertainment but for sustenance. Life is very different in a small provincial town, where the cook participates actively in her employer's social life.

In the small Normandy town of Alençon lives an old maid whose seductiveness relies entirely on her fortune. Mademoiselle Cormon, the heroine of Balzac's *An Old Maid*, is surrounded by suitors and reigns over the 150 people who constitute her usual company. Although obsessed with men and marriage, she cannot make up her mind to grant her hand to anyone, and consoles herself by focusing on the perfection of her household and the elegance of her weekly dinners. The food she serves is so excellent that Mademoiselle Cormon looks to her admirers like a "plump partridge," a mouth-watering incentive to gourmets' knives. On these gala evenings, the meal is served at four o'clock. The provinces were slow to change their habits: Balzac points out that under the Empire, people still dined at two o'clock, as they had done under the ancien régime.

"The dining-room, paved in black and white stone, not ceiled, and its beams painted, was furnished with one of those enormous sideboards with marble tops, required by the war waged in the provinces against the human stomach. The walls, painted in fresco, represented a flowery trellis. The seats were of varnished cane, and the doors of natural wood. All things about the place carried out the patriarchal air which emanated from the inside as well as the outside of the house. The genius of the provinces preserved everything; nothing was new or old, neither young nor decrepit."

These dinners bring together some twenty people and are sufficiently stuffy occasions for the seating to be indicated by small cards, but regulars stop briefly before going through to the drawing-room, to chat with Mariette, the cook, a great specialist of regional cuisine, who likes to comment on the menu for guests:

Mariette remarked to the chief-justice as he passed the kitchen: "Ah, Monsieur du Ronceret, I've cooked the cauliflowers au gratin expressly for you, for mademoiselle knows how you like them; and she said to me: 'Now don't forget, Mariette, for Monsieur du Ronceret is coming.'"

"That good Mademoiselle Cormon!" ejaculated the chief legal authority of the town. "Mariette, did you steep them in gravy instead of soupstock? It is much richer."

The chief-justice was not above entering the chamber of council where Mariette held court; he cast the eye of a gastronome around it, and offered the advice of a past master in cookery.

"Good-day, madam," said Josette to Madame Granson . . . , "Mademoiselle has thought of you, and there's fish for dinner."

As for the Chevalier de Valois, he remarked to Mariette in the easy tone of a great seigneur who condescends to be familiar: "Well, my dear cordon-bleu, to whom I should give the cross of the Legion of honor, is there some little dainty for which I had better reserve myself?"

"Yes, yes, Monsieur de Valois, a hare sent from Prebaudet; it weighs fourteen pounds."

Here we see the profound differences between Paris and the provinces. In Paris the aim of a dinner was to meet people. In an established household there would of course be regulars, but the well-advised hostess would always try to attract an unexpected—and therefore interesting—guest. The conversation would not always be the same, even less so with meals organized in restaurants. In the provinces there were no restaurants, so a person of standing had no way of sitting down to eat with someone outside his or her circle of acquaintances. Social divides were intractable, while in Paris social differences grew smaller by the day. In the town of Angoulême, when the most notable local figure, Madame de Bargeton, invites Lucien, the pharmacist's son, she causes a minor revolution. Old provincial nobility lived in an isolation that was unthinkable in Paris. Each person had a narrowly defined, unified society, quite distinct from society as a whole. And the provinces were immobile in the purest sense of the word: distance was still a great barrier at the time. In 1840 a stagecoach, a large public carriage that could transport sixteen passengers in unbearable discomfort, covered at best four to five leagues (ten to twelve miles) in an hour. Even then, allowances had to be made for changing horses, stopping to feed the passengers, and slowing down for hills or accidents. It took more than a day to travel the 120 miles between Paris and Alençon, and two days' journey to reach Tours, which is now one hour from Paris by train. News traveled slowly, exchanges were rare, and this was proved by the rhythm of life. People lived in an autarchy: they ate what the farmer raised and grew; they saw only their own family members and close friends, every evening, playing the same old backgammon and telling the same old jokes. In other words, life was quite boring.

Dinner, despite the often insipid conversation, was not only a meal but also a form of entertainment, a distraction which disrupted the dullness of everyday life. It assumed a degree of importance in itself, which was rarely the case in Paris. "In Paris people . . . trifle with their pleasure; in the provinces things are done naturally, and interest is perhaps rather too much concentrated on the grand and universal means of existence to which God has condemned his creatures."

These different cooks—Madame Rigou, Jacquotte, and Mariette—are faithful reflections of their respective masters' tyranny, goodness, and sociability, but we need to look quite separately at the staff employed by misers: Nanon, Monsieur Grandet's cook; and Gritte, Monsieur Hochon's servant. With them, cooking is not a question of gastronomy but of finding different ruses to keep spending to a strict minimum. Grandet and Harpagon share the dubious honor of being literary symbols of miserliness. Monsieur Hochon, a secondary character in *The Black Sheep*, is explored in less depth but has the advantage, for the purposes of this book, of revealing the most about himself at mealtimes. It is widely recognized that misers are rarely happy, but what is surprising is that in Balzac's work, food worshippers do not seem to be any more so.

THE MISERS
AND THE FOOD
WORSHIPPERS

We should eat to live and not live to eat, an admirable axiom adopted by all misers in *The Human Comedy*. And, although Balzac made a point of describing Grandet and Gobseck in detail and Hochon more fleetingly, he did not stint on sketching out plenty of others. They all share the same obsessive fear of food. In *The Muse of the Department*, Monsieur de la Baudraye scolds his wife for giving their friends brioche. To depict the savage parsimony of the Sauviats—the scrap metal merchants whose daughter Véronique is the heroine of *The Country Parson*—Balzac describes the despairing way the wife takes a coin from her apron to buy meat on high days and holidays; most of the time she and her husband make do with herrings, red lentils, cheese, and hard-boiled eggs mixed into salad. Their only provisions are a few onions or bulbs of garlic. On this diet they make a fortune. Their future son-in-law, Monsieur Graslin, who has also grown extremely rich, is so proverbially frugal that "in twenty-five years Graslin had not so much as offered a glass of water to any creature" because he feels so little need to be liked in society. But these traits are verging on caricature. The portraits of Gobseck, Grandet, and Hochon are far more detailed and individual, and the way they feed themselves and other people is a key element of their behavior.

The first two are terrible characters, the third more comic. Grandet takes miserliness and acquisitiveness to the point of robbery, abandoning his principles for the possibility of the smallest financial gain, passionate about gold for gold's sake. Grandet breaks the pact he has with local wine growers, betrays his nephew, swindles his wife and daughter, and, on his deathbed, has a hideous reflex to snatch the silver crucifix the priest holds over him. The moneylender Gobseck also worships gold, but in him Balzac created a very different and unusual character. Unlike Grandet, he has a mysterious and fairly eerie past. When he appears in *The Human Comedy* in the novel that bears his name, he is a usurer, a timeless and in some ways abstract profession, whereas Grandet is actually deeply rooted in the realities of everyday life. Grandet watches the weather: a cold spell could determine a loss or a gain for a country property, whereas Gobseck does not need to get out of his armchair to calculate how much he will earn from the diamonds that a society woman has entrusted to him. What the two men have in common is their obsession with, their almost physical love of, gold. This passion defines them, just as alchemy defines Balthasar Claes in *The Quest of the Absolute*, or as lust does Baron Hulot. By contrast, Monsieur Hochon does not have the same ambitions: we do not see him accumulating money, but suffering, oh so painfully, when he has to spend it.

Monsieur Hochon, a tax inspector for the ancien régime, escaped the turmoil of the Revolution and lives peacefully in Issoudun, in the heart of the Berry region. He is eighty-five years old when we meet him. Balzac does not beat around the bush: to portray him, he immediately relates the scene in which his cook interrupts him reading his daughter's wedding contract when she comes to ask for some string to truss the turkey. He takes an old shoelace from the pocket of his frock coat and says, "Give it back." The character is established, but what gives him his flavor is his attitude at mealtimes. He is a miser who thinks he can trick those around him with childish ploys. To his great displeasure, he finds himself constrained to hosting Agathe Bridau, his wife's goddaughter, accompanied by her son Joseph, a painter set to become a great artist, an artist very much to Balzac's taste, very gifted and hardworking and playful—as they could be in Paris studios. When he comes down for dinner on the day they arrive, Joseph notices the old man assiduously slicing bread in advance. We would have done better to stay at the inn, thinks the young man. He is not wrong there.

They are served soup, thin soup, of course. Clearly the quantity outstrips its quality. Gritte, the servant, then lays all the dishes on the table, as was the old custom. In more sophisticated households, boiled meat was usually presented surrounded by the vegetables used in cooking, and a second plate of fresh vegetables was offered to guests. Monsieur Hochon, though, resolves the problem to his advantage by serving the meat "triumphantly" surrounded by parsley, while the carrots, turnips, and onions used for stewing constitute a separate dish. There was also a salad of hard-boiled eggs with sorrel, and little pots of vanilla custard, except that "the vanilla was replaced by burned oats, which no more resembled vanilla than coffee made of chicory resembles genuine mocha." The master of the house cuts the meat into slices as thin as shoe soles. Boiled meat was not highly thought of by connoisseurs, but it took little preparation and was therefore practical in households that had to cope with only one servant. Next, Gritte brings in three pigeons. The old man's face reveals how painful this extravagance is to him, three pigeons for seven people—an extravagance his wife insisted on! As she had no say in the matter of wine, Monsieur Hochon serves his guests with his 1811 vintage, which is as good as saying it is undrinkable, because the harvest that year, the year of the comet, was ruined.

Joseph Bridau is young and hungry. He and his mother last ate at six o'clock in the morning in an awful café. The portions handed out only sharpen his appetite, so he asks for more bread.

"Monsieur Hochon rose, felt slowly for a key in the depths of his coat pocket, opened a cupboard behind him, took up a fragment of a twelve pound loaf, ceremoniously cut off another slice, broke it in two pieces, placed them on a plate and passed the plate across the table to the young painter, with the silent self-possession of an old soldier who says to himself at the beginning of battle: 'I may be killed today.' Joseph took half of the slice and understood that he must not ask again to be helped twice to bread. Not one member of the family expressed any surprise at this episode, monstrous as it seemed to Joseph."

There is worse to come. Small cheeses surrounded by walnuts and biscuits constitute the dessert. It is worth pointing out that walnuts were a poor man's food in Balzac's world, because all his life he would remember the mouselike meals, the suppers of bread and hazelnuts or bread and cherries, that he nibbled on in his student garret. Wanting to honor her guests, Madame Hochon asks for some fruit. "But, madam," replies Gritte, "there is no rotten fruit left." Joseph roars with laughter, realizing that the precaution of eating the ripest fruit first suffers no exceptions, and he assures his elderly hostess that he will eat some anyway.

Gobseck is a much more formidable character. He inspires dread. Doesn't a usurer's money come straight from other people's pockets? The man's beginnings are as mysterious as they are violent. He was born to a Dutch father and a Jewish mother. On his mother's orders, he enlisted as a ship's boy at the age of ten. He traveled the world for twenty years, and Balzac alludes to various horrible incidents, sudden terrors, and unhoped-for pleasures. After long stopovers in Dutch territories in the East Indies, he had a spell in Argentina, participated in the American War of Independence, and met the most famous privateers of the day . . . but his creator never explains how he ends up living in a miserable little room on the rue de Grès (now the rue Cujas) in the Latin Quarter, where he exercises his profession with peerless rigor and full knowledge of its risks. Balzac does not seem to make much of his Jewish origins; out of indifference or a lack of faith, Gobseck does not observe any religion and lives quite outside the Jewish community. In this he is little different from the other thirty or so Jewish characters in *The Human Comedy*. They are mostly either half Jews or only recently converted. They are never part of a group, a family, or a synagogue. Balzac never emphasizes their identity. They are assimilated. Gobseck, the picture seller Magus, and the banker Nucingen all exercise trades that have traditionally been viewed as Jewish, but plenty of others are journalists, doctors, or simply bystanders.

Gobseck's whole story, in the novella that bears his name, is told by his neighbor, the young attorney-at-law Derville, who is just starting out in life and will end up as the greatest attorney-at-law in *The Human Comedy*. Derville is fascinated by Gobseck, whose clients are wealthy young men, foolhardy society ladies, and bankers teetering on the brink of bankruptcy. He is inflexible and merciless, seeing through their every ruse, snapping back with perceptive one-liners that reduce them to powerless despair. He is emaciated and always alone, refusing any contact with his only relations, his sister's children and grandchildren (since in Balzac's world we end up knowing everyone, the reader soon discovers that Gobseck's last descendant is the famous courtesan, Esther). He is an extraordinary character, says Derville, because he knows everything. What magical powers does this "oyster beneath its rock" have that enable him to suspect intimate secrets and predict financial ruin before it is announced? Gobseck's economizing even runs to his own voice. He does not make the least sound, unlike his clients, or rather his victims, who "sometimes flew into a rage and made a great deal of noise; followed by a great silence; so is it in a kitchen after a fowl's neck has been wrung." He seems to feed off gold and precious stones. Derville watches him one day when the Comtesse de Restaud, Father Goriot's daughter, brings him her diamonds as security. "There was a flush in his pale cheeks; his eyes seemed to have caught the sparkle of the stones, for there was an unnatural glitter in them. He rose and went to the light, holding the diamonds close to his toothless mouth, as if he meant to devour them; mumbling vague words over them, holding up bracelets, sprays, necklaces, and tiaras one after another, to judge of their water, whiteness, and cutting; taking them out of the jewel-case and putting them in again, letting the play of the light bring out all their fires. He was more like a child than an old man; or, rather, childhood and dotage seemed to meet in him."

Does Gobseck eat anything other than diamonds? He is lean, thin, with spare vigorous limbs like a stag, feeding himself at home once a day on what the local roast meat seller delivers, and making do with coffee he prepares on a metal stand squeezed into a corner of the fireplace. Twice a week

Derville invites him for dinner, where he feasts on a partridge wing and a glass of champagne. It is in the dementia of old age that his relationship with food breaks down completely. He starts to insist that his debtors give him payment in kind; he stores up these provisions, but with the illogical instincts peculiar to some misers, does not use them. According to his doorkeeper, "he swallows it all and is none the fatter for it"— which is one of the frightening symptoms of "the childishness and incomprehensible obstinacy of age, a condition of mind reached at last by all men in whom a strong passion survives the intellect," and means that Balzac (who was no enemy to excess himself) has an opportunity to describe a rotting heap of rare and costly foods. Like an insatiable boa—Balzac compares Grandet to the same snake—Gobseck accepts his gifts and piles them up in rooms he has rented for this very purpose. Grandet, a logical man faithful to his passion for money, sells anything that he cannot or does not want to eat, while Gobseck, in his senility, quibbles with secondhand food traders, and while the discussions drag on, the merchandise rots.

Derville is summoned by the porter when Gobseck seems to be at death's door, and the old man, recognizing that he is weakening and "must leave everything," names Derville as the executor of his will, asks him to look for Esther, his young heiress, and even specifies that her nickname is La Torpille and she is the prettiest little thing. He gives Derville one final perplexing instruction: "take what you like; help yourself. There are Strasburg pâtés, there, and bags of coffee, and sugar, and gold spoons." Then, putting his bony hand over his blanket as if to hold himself down, he gives his last sigh. Disconcerted by these mad ramblings, Derville grabs the keys and goes into the neighboring rooms. In the first, he finds

a huge quantity of eatables of all kinds—putrid pies, mouldy fish, nay, even shell-fish, the stench almost choked me. Maggots and insects swarmed. These comparatively recent presents were put down, pell-mell, among chests of tea, bags of coffee, and packing-cases of every shape. A silver soup tureen on the chimney-piece was full of advices of the arrival of goods consigned to his order at Le Havre, bales of cotton, hogsheads of sugar, barrels of rum, coffees, indigo, tobaccos, a perfect bazaar of colonial produce . . . I went back to his room and found an explanation of this chaos and accumulation of riches in a pile of letters lying under the paper-weights on his desk—Gobseck's correspondence with the various dealers to whom doubtless he usually sold his presents. These persons had, perhaps, fallen victim to Gobseck's cleverness, or Gobseck may have wanted fancy prices for his goods; at any rate, every bargain hung in suspense. He had not disposed of the eatables to Chevet, because Chevet would only take them off him at a loss of thirty percent . . . Again, Gobseck had refused free delivery of his silverplate, and declined to guarantee the weights of his coffees. There had been a dispute over each article . . ."

Alongside this waste of food there is his wasted legacy. Gobseck dies the very day that the beautiful Esther commits suicide. His fortune will not have served him or anyone else. The miser's arid existence is encapsulated in his total denial of pleasure at mealtimes. But Gobseck lives alone and brings suffering only on himself, if indeed these privations make him suffer.

This is not the case with Monsieur Grandet, who is a social character, living in a family home surrounded by neighbors and supported by a genuine treasure, his servant Nanon, who deserves a place of honor in the gallery of Balzacian cooks. He is served like a despot by the three women in his household: his wife, his daughter, and his servant. When he goes to bed, everybody else is expected to go too, and his wife sleeps, eats, drinks, and moves to suit him. He terrifies her, and his daughter would never dare address him unless invited. Only

Nanon does not lose her composure when he looks at her; she has the confidence to cope with the daily sessions during which Monsieur Grandet discusses the contents of the larder with her, and she gauges the bread and produce for the day so as to ask him for a little extra, sometimes even sharing a joke. This is because Grandet trusts her and recognizes her intelligence. She is his agent, an agent who defends his best interests like a faithful dog, an agent who does everything, waking early and retiring late, and one whose authority is recognized by his stupid wife and idiotic daughter. It is Nanon and not Madame Grandet who collects the farmers' rents in the master's absence. It is to Nanon that he gives responsibility for his funds in a secret operation.

How does he run his household? He has stripped his wife of all responsibility for it, deeming her incapable of understanding his principles. So he alone oversees how their daily menus are formulated. His fundamental theory is simple: never take a single sou from your pocket, in other words buy nothing. Even people of the most modest means buy their bread from a baker, but in Monsieur Grandet's household, bread is baked at home once a week. He never buys red meat, and his household would thrive perfectly happily on capons, chicken, game, river fish, eels and pike, eggs, and fruit owed by tenant farmers if he did not immediately sell everything except what is strictly necessary. Is there any need to point out that they eat little in the Grandet household? If they need to make stock, they kill a crow. Each person is entitled to one piece of sugar a day, a very small piece. It is Monsieur Grandet himself who takes pleasure in cutting it up in his spare time, because sugar is still sold in loaves. Under the Restoration, its price had dropped, because there was now free trading for cane sugar, and beet sugar had come on the market; sugar was becoming widely available, but, to Monsieur Grandet, it is still a great luxury, just as coffee is. Coffee had actually been the most widespread drink in France for some time, across every social class. When the marketplace opened at Les Halles, women carried tin-plate urns of coffee on their backs and poured it into little earthenware cups for passersby. Sugar was not a dominant feature of coffee, but milk sweetened it enough for it to have become the first comfort of the day for all workmen. Even Monsieur Grandet does not dare deprive his family of this drink, but Nanon has orders to serve it very weak.

What do they actually eat in the Grandet household then? A cup of coffee on waking and virtually nothing at eleven o'clock. They do not even sit down. Food affords no pleasure whatsoever. They have lunch on their feet, snacking on a piece of fruit or a hunk of bread and a glass of white wine. It is

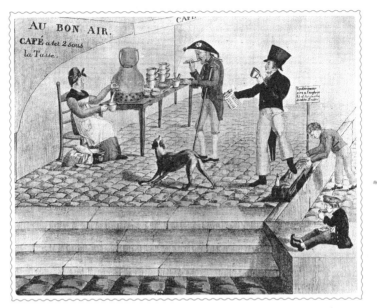

Parisians drank coffee all day and could buy a cup anywhere in the city.

important to realize that wine cost nothing in Saumur and was as readily available there as tea in India. Dinner consists of some soup and a bit of chicken apart from very exceptional occasions when Monsieur Grandet has guests. And when I say exceptional, I mean four times in twenty years! Then he is quite capable of producing excellent wines from his cellar (the treasures lurking in Balzacian wine cellars are inexhaustible) and asking for game and fish to be prepared, but he is equally capable of going twenty-four hours without food if he has to be away from home.

This monastic regime—which must have some constitutional advantages because no one is ever ill in his household—eventually seems quite normal to the family until the arrival of the Parisian cousin, Charles, a young man of rare elegance. Charles turns up one evening unannounced, sent by his father. He does not know that the latter has just gone bankrupt and shot himself in the head. Monsieur Grandet learns the news when he reads the sealed letter that his nephew hands him on arrival, and does not betray a thing. Everyone goes to bed, but the following day Eugénie, touched or rather bowled over by her cousin's looks, is determined to improve the household's ordinary fare. She is quite sure he is not used to making do with a cup of coffee on waking, but whatever else can she offer him? She confides her plan to Nanon, clearly horrified at the thought of asking her father for anything; as soon as Monsieur Grandet has left to attend to business, the women busy themselves and Nanon agrees to go and buy sugar and coffee with the few coins Eugénie can spare from her savings.

The handsome young man rises at last, and the comedy begins. What would he like to eat? Oh, nothing. Perhaps a partridge or a chicken. Nanon does not lose her cool and offers him two boiled eggs given to her by a farmer, some prettily arranged grapes, and a cup of milky coffee, next to which Eugénie has put a saucer with several pieces of sugar. And she has set up a small table by the fireplace and drawn an armchair up to the fire to make the living room more welcoming. The cousin is delighted with his fresh eggs but the coffee is so bad it makes him laugh. Nanon may well have increased the dosage, but Grandet coffee is little more than colored water.

The Grandets are still boiling their coffee, which makes it cloudy, at a time when all of France was taking to the Chaptal *cafetière*, made of two receptacles separated by a filter. (Balzac preferred the Dubelloy model, which could make particularly strong filter coffee, likely to produce a state of nervous excitement, according to Alexandre Dumas.) But—catastrophe—Monsieur Grandet's footsteps are heard. Madame Grandet stiffens like a terrified doe, and Eugénie withdraws the saucer, leaving only two pieces of sugar on the table. Nanon snatches away the plate of eggs. In vain. Grandet takes in the whole scene, freezes his wife with a stony stare, and expresses astonishment that his daughter should challenge him by daring to turn around and offer him some grapes, but it does not take him long to restore order in the house. Charles soon has to comply with the discipline imposed by his uncle.

Many will know how the story ends. Charles sets off to make a new fortune in the Indies and Eugénie gives him her savings, in gold coins, to help him start out. When her father discovers she has done this, he flies into a rage and condemns his daughter to bread and water. The denouement is as sad as could be predicted: Madame Grandet dies and Eugénie, who has never had any news from Charles, lives on alone with her father. He eventually recognizes that he has indoctrinated her with his ferociously economical ways and need fear nothing in surrendering the running of the house to her. He withers and has a stroke that leaves him paralyzed. He barely eats a thing but can sit for hours on end looking at the gold coins that Eugénie spreads out on the table for him: "'That warms me!' he muttered more than once, and his face expressed a perfect content."

Was he thinking back to the past when he fed off coins? In his heyday, "[i]n matters financial M Grandet might be described as combining the characteristics of a Bengal tiger and the boa constrictor. He could lie low and wait, crouching, watching for his prey, and make his spring, unerringly at last; then the jaws of his purse would unclose, a torrent of coin would be swallowed down, and, as in the case of the gorged reptile, there would be a period of inaction; like the serpent, moreover, he was cold, apathetic, methodical, keeping to his own mysterious times and seasons." That is the miser's only true food.

*J*N CONTRAST to the great misers who would rather eat gold than anything else, food lovers have a more traditional view of the pleasures to be had at table. I am talking here specifically of food-loving men, because society women eat little in novels from this period. Maupassant stated that they were incapable of experiencing the pleasure afforded by a great wine, even though a few exceptions did respect good cooking. In Balzac's work, only the Princess of Cadignan understands that, in order to seduce Daniel d'Arthez, who loathes affectation, she would do well to abandon the exaggerations of a strict diet, behaving naturally and eating heartily. But most of the women are too afraid of gaining weight to abandon restraint at mealtimes.

> Women eat little at a formal dinner: their concealed harness hampers them, they are laced tightly, and they are in the presence of women whose eyes and whose tongues are equally to be dreaded. They prefer fancy eating to good eating, then: they will suck a lobster's claw, swallow a quail or two, punish a woodcock's

wing, beginning with a bit of fresh fish, flavored by one of those sauces which are the glory of French cooking. France is everywhere sovereign in matters of taste: in painting, fashions, and the like. Gravy is the triumph of taste, in cookery. So that grisettes, shopkeepers' wives and duchesses are delighted with a tasty little dinner washed down with the choicest wines, of which, however, they drink but little, the whole concluded by fruit such as can only be had at Paris; and especially delighted when they go to the theatre to digest the little dinner, and listen, in a comfortable box, to the nonsense uttered upon the stage, and to that whispered in their ears to explain it."

Men, as we have seen, have none of this daintiness, but oddly, it is hard to find a happy food lover in *The Human Comedy*. It is no accident that the characters who love food are often priests, who are forbidden the pleasures of love, or men cuckolded by their wives, those scorned by people around them, those miserable because they have little success with the ladies, or those who are simply bored. Balzac likes to connect misfortunes in bed and pleasure at table. This is because, to him, a delight in food is often a compensation. Women actually play on their husband's or lover's greediness, and quickly learn that they get better results by offering a treat in reparation rather than as bait. This is how Balzac envisages the former in *The Physiology of Marriage*:

> Suppose that conjugal misfortune has fallen upon an epicure. He naturally demands the consolations which suit his taste. His sense of pleasure takes refuge in other gratifications, and forms other habits. You shape your life in accordance with the enjoyment of other sensations.
>
> One day, returning from your government office, after lingering for a long time before [Chevet's shelves stacked with delicious riches], hovering in suspense between the hundred francs of expense, and the joy [promised by] a Strasbourg *pâté de fois gras*, you are struck dumb on finding this *pâté* proudly installed on the sideboard of your dining-room. Is this vision offered by some gastronomic mirage? In this doubting mood you approach with firm step, for a *pâté* is a living creature, and [you] seem to neigh as you scent afar off the truffles whose perfumes escape through the gilded enclosure. You stoop over it two distinct times; all the nerve centres of your palate have a soul; you taste the delights of a genuine feast, etc.; and during this ecstasy

a feeling of remorse seizes upon you, and you go to your wife's room.

"Really, my dear girl, we have not means which warrant our buying *pâtés*."

"But it costs us nothing!"

"Oh! ho!"

"Yes, it is M. Achille's brother who sent it to him."

You catch sight of M. Achille in a corner. The [bachelor] greets you, he is radiant on seeing that you have accepted the *pâté*. You look at your wife, who blushes; you stroke your beard a few times; and, as you express no thanks, the two lovers divine your acceptance of the compensation.

As if the pâté were not enough, his wife adopts the behavior of an odalisque when serving him his evening coffee: "she strains [his favorite brew] with special care, sweetens it, tastes it, and hands it to him . . . with a smile." And there, according to Balzac, is a happy epicurean.

Women very rarely manage to secure a man through his stomach. Only one succeeds: Madame Schontz. This Napoleonic colonel's daughter and goddaughter to the Empress Josephine is well brought up but has no money. She earns a living teaching young children at Saint-Denis, a school founded by

Napoleon, for girls whose father or grandfather was decorated with the Légion d'Honneur. But she tires of the institution's austerity and launches into the world of courtesans. Success is a long time coming because she is older than her "colleagues." She seizes her chance when she meets Arthur de Rochefide, who has been cruelly abandoned by his wife Beatrix. He is as tight-fisted as he is distrustful and gives her only twelve hundred francs a month, but Aurélie Schontz is cunning. She will win Arthur de Rochefide with her cooking and her economizing. He can easily spend sixty francs every time he goes to a restaurant, and more than two hundred the moment he invites two or three friends. She offers to make dinner for him and his friends every evening for forty francs. When he gladly accepts, she asks for more money to buy dresses so that he need not feel ashamed in front of friends, all of whom are members of the Jockey Club.

Aurélie "contrived to display new virtues in this second phase. She laid out for herself a house-keeping role for which she claimed much credit. She made, so she said, both ends meet at the close of the month on two thousand five hundred francs without a debt,—a thing unheard of in the faubourg Saint-Germain of the 13th arrondissement,*—and she served

* At the time Paris had only twelve arrondissements (or districts). Anyone living in sin was said to be lodged in the thirteenth.

dinners infinitely superior to those of Nucingen, at which exquisite wines were drunk at twelve francs a bottle. Rochefide, amazed, and delighted to be able to invite his friends to the house with economy, declared, as he caught her round the waist, 'She's a treasure!'"

Madame Schontz wins the game, unlike poor Sabine du Guénic, who becomes aware of her husband Calyste's increasing indifference as he succumbs to the wife of the very same Monsieur de Rochefide, the intimidating Beatrix. Calyste is young, good-looking, weak, and spoiled. Beatrix feels she is near the upper age limit to be a seductress, which only increases her determination. Still very beautiful, adept in matters of love, and jealous of other people's happiness, she succeeds in breaking up the young couple. When Sabine notices that Calyste "would motion to the servants to take away his plate after pecking at two or three mouthfuls" instead of eating with his usual appetite, she thinks she will be able to win him back with food, and decides to  find out which dishes he enjoys with his mistress. Her faithful servant, Gasselin, "consort[ed] with Madame de Rochefide's cook, and before long, Sabine gave Calyste the same fare, only better; but still he made difficulties." Heartbroken by her husband's growing coldness, she takes it into her head that her rival provides the young man with "Indian sauces they serve in England in cruets. Madame de Rochefide accustoms him to all sorts of condiments." There is no need to add that it will take the ramifications of a quite different strategy to bring Calyste back to the fold, because it is not through his stomach or even aphrodisiac beetles that Madame de Rochefide holds him. Calyste is a happy lover, and therefore pays little attention to what is on his plate. A plot concocted by Sabine's mother, two devoted friends, and Aurélie Schontz will save the neglected wife. A destitute Italian count, La Palferina, accepts a generous payment in exchange for seducing Beatrix (a project facilitated by her vanity) and for making it widely known. Calyste then has a gauge of his mistress's depravity and comes back to his wife.

The truly greedy, as I have said above, never triumph. In *Albert Savarrus*, the gentleman Monsieur de Watteville (such a quiet character that Balzac compares him to a wood louse hidden in a rotting board), marries a wealthy heiress who is pious, gloomy, prudish, and prickly. It goes without saying that the household is far from cheerful. Monsieur de Watteville, a dry, crassly ignorant character with no wit, realizes very early on in the marriage that he will never hold sway over his wife. To console himself, he starts collecting insects and seashells, and focuses on the food he eats. In his house "the food was exquisite. The wines selected by Monsieur de Watteville, who, to occupy his time and vary his employments, was his own butler, enjoyed a sort of fame throughout the department." The minor glory achieved in this way is still not enough to brighten his existence, but preparing ceremonial dinners does help pass the time.

Another unhappy husband, the Comte de Monpersan, whose wife cheats on him, becomes as good as bulimic. To the astonishment of one of his visitors, he stays at the table and carries on eating while a crisis unfolds around him. His wife has disappeared and there are fears she has tried to drown herself. True, the countess's despair is provoked by the accidental death of her lover, but this does not excuse her husband's composure. "The ferocious hunger familiar to convalescents, sheer animal appetite, had overpowered all human sensibilities."

Of all the husbands in dysfunctional marriages who console themselves with food, we need to give special mention to Monsieur de Beauséant. The Parisian Vicomte de Beauséant is far too elegant to be pained by his wife's passion for the beautiful Marquis d'Ajuda-Pinto, who is a star "among the gilded and insolent youth of that period." For one thing, in their circles, sexual fidelity is viewed more as a source of ridicule than a virtue; for another, he is delighted that the lover's presence releases him from having to accompany his wife to the theater

Oysters were ordered by the hundred.

in the evening. Monsieur de Beauséant is fundamentally blasé and "had few pleasures left but those of good cheer." Like his king, Louis XVIII, who was so fond of food he allowed himself to grow too fat to stand without support, he adheres to a double luxury when it comes to eating: "the luxury of style and that of content." His dining room therefore glories in all the luxuries associated with mealtimes that "in the time of the Restoration . . . were carried to the highest degree." Indeed the aesthetics of gastronomy reached a pinnacle in this period. Like Balzac himself, the vicomte is charmed by magnificent sculpted silverware, incomparably fine linen, silent staff, and an absence of vulgar smells that might corrupt the aroma of each dish. He insists on perfect presentation. Pleasure for the eyes takes precedence over the actual taste. There is no doubting that Monsieur de Beauséant's chef follows Carême's example in garnishing dishes with truffles cut into petal shapes, oysters hidden in nests of seaweed, different-colored aspic, tiny constructions made with cabbage, spinach, and lettuce leaves and held up with buntings' beaks. Fruits and vegetables can appear only as decorative mousses. Everything is masked, complex, and subtle. It is hardly surprising that the suppers that, under the Empire, followed a ball (because "officers who took part in them must be fortified for immediate service" either on or off the battlefield!) seem crude to the vicomte, with their mountains of ham, sausages, boar's heads, and still bloody meat. The Restoration, a period that Balzac particularly liked, reintroduced a degree of refinement, more delicate tastes, and daintier manners, in direct contrast to the previous regime, which favored power and energy—a change of sensibilities reflected in the art of presenting a meal. It is

Monsieur de Beauséant who gives Rastignac (still a poor student in the *Father Goriot* days) a glimpse of absolute luxury, poetic luxury. But these characters—Watteville, Monpersan, and Beauséant—are merely sketches of epicureans, unlike the finely honed Rouget father and son in *The Black Sheep*, or Cousin Pons, whose love of food proves fatal.

The Black Sheep is one of the darkest, most incident-packed, and most dramatic of Balzac's novels. A multitude of characters vie for center stage and take the reader from Paris to Issoudun with a detour via America. We met one of them earlier: the elderly miser, Monsieur Hochon. Now let us turn our attention to Dr. Rouget and his son, both settled in Issoudun and both very fond of food, each in his own way and for very different reasons.

The first is a "malicious, evil-minded old man," the second a boy who is perfectly useless. On the way back from one of his rounds, the doctor notices a very pretty young girl in ragged clothes, stirring* the water in a stream to frighten crayfish, drive them upstream, and make it easier for a man waiting to catch them. The doctor stops and talks to her and, when he learns that she is twelve years old, he asks whether she would like to go home with him. You will be well fed, well clothed,

---

* In Balzac's original novel the verb used for this stirring is *rabouiller* and the girl doing it is called *la rabouilleuse*, which gives the work its title.

and I will give you pretty shoes, he promises in order to persuade her. To conclude the deal, he offers the man with her—who is her uncle—the tidy sum of two hundred écus.

Once back at his house, the girl, whose name is Flore, is given a quick wash and told she can sleep in the room above his. He summons a seamstress and a cobbler to make Flore presentable; later he gives her a tutor to teach her to read and count. The doctor sees himself as a small-scale Louis XV (Louis XV often spent his evenings with a troupe of very young girls in a private house, the Parc aux Cerfs), and takes delight in preparing what he believes will be the perfect complement to pleasant evenings in the not-too-distant future. But at seventy, he feels he is "in the flower of old age," and when the time comes to pick the fruit he has to concede that "nature had foiled the schemes of his lust." Nevertheless, Flore stays in the house, where she feels extremely lucky, particularly when she compares her life to the one she would be living with her uncle. She does not even recoil from complying with some of the doctor's requests, "as an Eastern slave would have done," thinking—with a good dose of peasant common sense—that anything that might release her from "the hellish round of hunger and everlasting toil" is legitimate. With his customary skill and without going into detail, Balzac gives glimpses of damage done.

Nevertheless, this failure (which is exacerbated by the young girl's beauty) eats away at the doctor, and he turns to food for consolation. His meals are of remarkable quality, thanks to the talents of Fanchette, the fat servant from the Berry region whom he himself trained, and because he had cleverly managed to apply his knowledge of chemistry—learned while he was studying medicine in Paris—to culinary art. Perhaps this is why he is responsible for the only recipe in *The Human Comedy*.

"He is renowned at Issoudun for several improvements in the art of cooking, little known outside of Berry. He discovered that an omelette is more delicate when the whites and yolks of the eggs are not beaten together with the brutality that cooks usually put into that operation. According to him, the white should be beaten until it resembles foam and the yolk introduced a little at a time, and you should not use a frying-pan, but a *cagnard* made of porcelain or earthenware. The *cagnard* is a sort of [platter] with four feet so that, when it is put on the stove, the air circulates underneath and prevents the heat from cracking it . . . The doctor had also found a way to kill the acrid taste of [a flour sauce]; but that secret, which unluckily he confined to his kitchen, has been lost."

His table is not one that sees great gatherings of friends. Rouget is disliked by the locals; he frightens his neighbors and those around him. People know that he made his wife unhappy and was unjustifiably hard on his daughter. He is difficult, people say, though they smile sweetly when they meet him but gossip about his reputation for debauchery:

> "What do you suppose that old ape means to do with a girl of fifteen—a man of his age?" someone would say, two years after the advent of La Rabouilleuse.
>
> "You are right," would be the reply, "his [heyday has] long gone by." . . .
>
> "Look you, the old rascal has read the Old Testament, if only as a doctor, and he has learned how King David warmed up his old age."

Despite the young girl's presence, then, his household is not a cheery place. His son, Jean-Jacques, is such an imbecile that he is poor company, and Flore's presence is a constant irritant. Dr. Rouget is yet another character we do not feel inclined to share a meal with.

The importance of food in this novel is not restricted to the doctor. When he dies, Flore becomes Jean-Jacques's mistress; this great witless lump is hopelessly in love with her and she takes over running the house with authority and competence. She has watched Fanchette very closely because she wanted to be able to replace her or train another servant, guessing that the old cook would not stay in the house under her direction. Flore then has total power over Jean-Jacques, who, with his utterly empty life, relies on her for his every pleasure. "Mademoiselle Brazier [Flore] placed the table upon an Episcopal footing. Rouget, being thus led into the way of high living, ate more and more . . . But, despite the large quantities of nourishing food that he consumed, he gained but little flesh. From day to day he failed visibly, like a man who was completely tired out,—by the labor of digestion perhaps,—and there were deep black rings about his eyes." He falls asleep, snoring after dinner every day. In one generation, the family has toppled from the gourmet to the glutton. The father's appetite, the epicurean greed of a connoisseur, certainly afforded him some consolation; but the son's gluttony proves fatal, and he dies of acute indigestion brought on by a slice of pâté de foie gras.

Young Rouget's death fits perfectly within Balzac's philosophy that any form of excess should cut life short. The novelist remained very close to the theories put forward by his own father, who, it is worth reiterating, never ate in the evening and constantly propounded the dangers of eating too well, because "the brain is atrophied (as it were), [and] a second brain, located in the diaphragm, may come into play . . . What man, on the wrong side of forty, is rash enough to work after dinner? And remark in the same connection, that all great men have been moderate eaters." I can hardly stress enough how severely Balzac judges his greedier characters. These obsessive food lovers do not really live well or to the fullest, and those who are not actually evil are slaves to their own mania. Cousin Pons, the most notable food lover in *The Human Comedy*, does not die of excess but of sorrow. Yet all his sorrows derive from his consuming obsession with food.

Cousin Pons is a true food lover, quite lip-smackingly so. He is no cook, does not claim the least technical knowledge, and has never had to guide a chef or to cook for himself. He has always eaten in other people's houses. From the first time we see him, we watch him "walking along the Boulevard des Italiens with his head bent down, as if he were tracking someone. There was a smug expression about the mouth—he looked like a merchant who has just done a good stroke of business, or a bachelor emerging from a boudoir in the best of humors with himself." He is not emerging from a boudoir at all, but anticipating an excellent dinner with his cousin, Camusot de Marville, who is the presiding judge at the Court Chambers.

Sylvain Pons is a talented musician and charming composer whose hour of glory came under the Empire. He is a good man with a heart of gold, a "tender, dreamy, sensitive soul." In his youth he improvised romances, composed a few operas, arranged concerts, and was so frequently invited out to dinner that he made a note of his invitations, "much as barristers note down the cases for which they are retained." Yes, he has a career as a musician, but his two predominant passions are eating and bric-a-brac, or, to be more accurate, ferreting out underpriced paintings and objets d'art. This second compulsion of Pons's is a secret: no one, apart from a rare few traders, knows about the extraordinary collection he has gathered over the years. The first is public and eventually causes him endless difficulties. Pons's taste for good food is the driving force in the novel.

Where did his ferocious greediness come from? Balzac offers a very simple explanation: Pons has never been smiled at by a woman, and this is hardly surprising. How could he hope to appeal to women, with "a countenance which was flattened something after the fashion of a pumpkin, and surmounted by a Don Quixote nose that rose out of it like a monolith above a plain"?

Plenty of men are doomed to this fate. Pons was an abnormal birth; the child of parents well stricken in years, he bore the stigma of his untimely genesis; his cadaverous complexion might have been contracted in the flask of spirit-of-wine in which science preserves some extraordinary foetus. Artist though he was . . . he was forced to accept the character which belonged to his face; it was hopeless to think of love, and he remained a bachelor, not so much of choice as of necessity. Then Gluttony, the sin of the continent monk, beckoned to Pons; he rushed upon temptation, as he had thrown his whole soul into the adoration of art and the cult of music. Good cheer and bric-a-brac gave him the small change for the love which could spend itself in no other way. As for music, it was his profession, and where will you find the man who is in love with his means of earning a livelihood? For it is with a profession as with marriage: in the long length you are sensible of nothing but the drawbacks.

While he is fashionable, this sin brings him nothing but pleasure: he eats out in town every evening. He is feted everywhere and offered things Balzac dreamed of as he sat chained to his desk: green beans, peas, and strawberries in season, and the most succulent fruit; his hosts uncork their best wines, perfect their desserts, coffee, and liqueurs, and pamper him as best they can, as guests were treated in "times of the Empire when Paris was glutted with kings and queens and princes, and many a private house emulated royal splendors."

When the novel opens, in 1844, Pons has reached the age of sixty. And these sixty years are hard to bear because surely being ugly and poor means "being three times as old." His work is no longer in favor and he is reduced to giving piano lessons in girls' boarding schools and conducting the orchestra in a second-rate theater. He often arrives uninvited at friends' houses at dinnertime, as close family members still did in those days, but he is given an unenthusiastic welcome. Each family accepts him "much as they accepted the taxes." Having been a perpetual guest, our Pons has become a scrounger. He is perfectly well aware of this but finds it impossible to make the transition from these generously laden tables to the insipid gruel of some forty-sous restaurant. "Alas! A shudder ran through him at the mere thought of the great sacrifices which independence required him to make. He felt that he was capable of sinking to even lower depths for the sake of good living, if there was no other way of enjoying the first and best of everything, of guzzling (vulgar but expressive word) nice little dishes carefully prepared. Pons lived like a bird, pilfering his meal, flying away when he had taken his fill, singing a few notes by way of return; he took a certain pleasure in the thought that he lived at the expense of society, which asked of him—what but the trifling toll of grimaces? . . . All through those years he contrived to dine without expense by making himself necessary in the houses which he frequented. He took the first step in the downward path by undertaking a host of small commissions; many and many a time Pons ran on errands instead of the porter or the servant." He is asked to buy small gifts and entrusted with confidences. He is so discreet that people forget he is there and talk in front of him quite openly. "[H]e became a kind of harmless, well-meaning spy, sent by one family into another; but he gained no credit with those for whom he trudged about, and so often sacrificed self-respect."

Pons stoops so low that his cousin's chambermaid takes it into her head to marry him, but he wants none of this squalid happiness. And anyway, he does not live alone. Pons has a friend, a friend who is so close and intimate that, Balzac tells us, "Pons contracted the only marriage that society would allow him—he married a man, an elderly man, a musician like himself." This character, who props him up through his old age, is called Schmucke. He is German, German like Mozart but without the audacity it takes to be a genius. This gentle, unselfish, naive man, who was formerly a choirmaster for the margrave in Anspach, meets Pons when he has been living in Paris—with his cat, Mirr—for twenty years, giving piano lessons to all the young ladies in *The Human Comedy*. They get along so well that they decide to move in together. Schmucke is an absentminded dreamer with modest tastes, quite happy to have a light snack at lunchtime and make do with whatever the porter, Madame Cibot, has cooked up for dinner; while Pons still goes out every evening.

When Pons admits to him the indignities he has to suffer, and how harshly he is often treated by his hosts, the good Schmucke recommends living as he does off bread and cheese at home, rather than going and eating other people's dinners, for which they make him pay so dearly. Alas! Pons dare not confess to Schmucke "that heart and stomach were at war within him, that he could digest affronts which pained his heart, and, cost what it might, a good dinner that satisfied his palate was a necessity to him, even as your gay Lothario must have a mistress to tease."

It is a striking parallel, and Balzac pursues this comparison between the gourmet, the über-foodie, and men obsessed with women. "A stomach thus educated is sure to react upon the owner's moral fibre; the demoralization of the man varies directly with his progress in culinary sapience. Voluptuousness, lurking in every secret recess of the heart, lays down the law therein. Honor and resolution are battered in breach. The tyranny of the palate has never been described; as a necessity of life it escapes the criticism of literature." And this does not surprise us, because, to Balzac, the joys of food were perfectly comparable to those of love:

> Brillat-Savarin has deliberately set himself to justify the gastronome, but perhaps even he has not dwelt sufficiently on the reality of the pleasures of the table. The demands of digestion upon the human economy produce an internal wrestling-bout of human forces which rivals the highest degree of amorous pleasure . . . The exhilarating effect of the wing of a chicken upon invalids recovering from serious illness, and long confined to a stinted and carefully chosen diet, has been frequently remarked. The sober Pons, whose whole enjoyment was concentrated in the exercise of his digestive organs, was in the position of chronic convalescence; he looked to his dinner to give him the utmost degree of pleasurable sensation, and hitherto he had procured such sensations daily. Who dares to bid farewell to old habit? Many a man on the brink of suicide has been plucked back on the threshold of death by the thought of the cafe where he plays his nightly game of dominoes.

Nevertheless, Pons is so appallingly treated by one of his relations, Madame Camusot de Marville, who is embittered by the difficulties she is having marrying off her daughter, that he renounces the wonderful carp that constitutes the main attraction in that household, and withdraws before dinner is served. He therefore returns home unexpectedly. Schmucke cannot contain his joy and, to console him, orders a fine meal from the Cadran Bleu: stewed veal, a fish dish, a good bottle of Bordeaux, and rice croquettes with smoked bacon, which he rather mysteriously describes as the greatest delicacy. Cue the arrival of the concierge, Madame Cibot, drawn by Pons's unexpected return and sniffing out the possibility of a good deal. Once she understands the situation, she eagerly agrees to cook them dinner every evening, although she grasps that she will have to make an extra effort if she is to satisfy her new client. So Pons leaves the realms of great cuisine to explore the delights of small-time city food, cobbled together out of small potatoes. He likes it, because he is enough of a connoisseur to taste it, but after having dinner alone with Schmucke for some three months he descends into a state of melancholy.

First, he does his sums: he now has to subtract eighty francs a month from the money he sets aside for buying works of art (because, on top of the forty-five francs Madame Cibot's dinners are costing him, he has to add about thirty-five francs for wine).

And very soon, in spite of all that Schmucke could do, in spite of his little German jokes, Pons fell to regretting the delicate dishes, the liqueurs, the good coffee, the table talk, the insincere politeness, the guests, and the gossip, and the houses where he used to dine. On the wrong side of sixty a man cannot break himself of a habit of thirty-six years' growth. Wine at a hundred and thirty francs per hogshead is scarcely a generous liquid in a *gourmet's* glass; every time that Pons raised it to his lips he thought, with infinite poignant regret, of the exquisite wines in his entertainers' cellars.

In short, at the end of three months, the cruel pangs which had gone near to break Pons' sensitive heart had died away; he forgot everything but the charms of society; and languished for them like some elderly slave of a petticoat compelled to leave the mistress who too repeatedly deceives him!

Balzac, who always thought of his characters as living people, must have been thinking of Baron Hulot, who, when confronted with Valérie Marneffe's duplicity, still clung to her petticoats. He only let go when she succeeded in ruining him and sent him home to his family.

Although he tries to conceal the profound melancholy consuming him, the aging Pons clearly succumbs to one of those inexplicable illnesses rooted in morale.

A single symptom will throw light upon this case of nostalgia (as it were) produced by breaking away from an old habit; in itself it is trifling, one of the myriad nothings which are as rings in a coat of chain-mail enveloping the soul in a network of iron. One of the keenest pleasures of Pons' old life, one of the joys of the dinner-table parasite at all times, was the "surprise," the thrill produced by the extra dainty dish added triumphantly to the bill of fare by the mistress of a bourgeois house, to give a festive air to the dinner. Pons' stomach hankered after that gastronomical satisfaction. Mme. Cibot, in the pride of her heart, enumerated every dish beforehand; a salt and savor once periodically recurrent, had vanished utterly from daily life. Dinner proceeded without *le plat couvert*, as our grandsires called it. This lay beyond the bounds of Schmucke's powers of comprehension. Pons had too much delicacy to grumble; but if the case of unappreciated genius is hard, it goes harder still with the stomach whose claims are ignored . . . Nothing can be compared to its sufferings; for, in the first place, one must live. Pons thought wistfully of certain creams—surely the poetry of cookery!—of certain white sauces, masterpieces of the art; of truffled chickens, fit to melt your heart; and above these, and more than all these, of the famous Rhine carp, only known at Paris, served with what condiments! There were days when Pons, thinking upon Count Popinot's cook, would sigh aloud, "Ah, Sophie!" Any passer-by hearing the exclamation might have thought that the old man referred to a lost mistress . . . The conductor of the orchestra, living on memories of past dinners, grew visibly leaner; he was pining away, a victim to gastric nostalgia.

One event brightens this sad period: the engagement dinner for the orchestra's flautist, a young German who is marrying the daughter of the Hôtel du Rhin's owner, Monsieur Graff. The latter, who was originally from Frankfurt, is delighted with the match and makes full use of his excellent connections with the best suppliers in Paris to lay on a sumptuous meal. Pons and Schmucke have never known such fare, delicate ingredients cooked simply but perfectly. "The dishes were a rapture to think of! Italian pasta, delicate of flavor, unknown to the public; smelts fried as never smelts were fried before; fish from Lake Leman, with a real Genevese sauce, and a cream for plum-pudding which would have astonished the London doctor who is said to have invented it." This English dessert had been in fashion for a number of years and required a lot of work and a long cooking time. Only the best cooks could master it. The dinner lasts until ten o'clock at night. "The amount of wine, German and French, consumed at that dinner would amaze the contemporary dandy; nobody knows the amount of liquor that a German can imbibe and yet keep calm and quiet; to have even an idea of the quantity, you must dine in Germany and watch bottle succeed to bottle, like wave rippling after wave along the sunny shores of the Mediterranean, and disappear as if the Teuton possessed the absorbing power of sponges or sea sand. Perfect harmony prevails meanwhile; there is none of the racket that there would be over the liquor in France; the talk is as sober as a money-lender's extempore speech; countenances flush, like the faces of the brides in frescoes by Cornelius or Schnorr (imperceptibly, that is to say), and reminiscences are poured out slowly while the smoke puffs from the pipes."

Sadly, the book does not close on this idyllic note and the soothing effect of good food. Pons is so gripped by the irresistible urge to dine out that he takes it into his head to be reconciled with Madame Camusot by finding a husband for her daughter, who is going to seed. The husband is to be the aforementioned flautist's best friend, another German, who has just inherited four million francs. It turns out that this Fritz would like to marry but knows no one in Paris and loathes making any effort or going to the trouble of courting. Someone will have to find the young lady for him. Pons seizes his chance and speaks highly of the candidate to the Camusot family. The strategy seems to work, and Pons is back in the parents' favor when, catastrophically, the German declines on the surprising grounds that the young lady is an only child and he is convinced that only children are always spoiled and unbearable. Madame Camusot's fury then falls on the unfortunate Pons, whom she accuses of betrayal, and the poor man literally dies of sorrow.

The moral of the story is that Pons's fascination with gastronomical delights—for that is unquestionably his motivation in everything—is an obsession, and is fatal like all Balzacian obsessions. Pons is no longer a man but a stomach, and he destroys himself as Hulot and Balthazar Claes destroy themselves, as victims of their obsessive passions. When pushed to extremes, any source of pleasure—be it women, intellectual pursuit, or food—leads to disaster. In *Cousin Pons*, gourmandise is not an indulgent partiality, not an appreciation of taste, but quite simply an illness.

It would be too sad to finish this chapter about food lovers on such a gloomy note. Are there really no happy, cheerful gluttons? Yes, but they are young and poor and their banquets are imaginary. They are the heroes of a lesser-known but extremely entertaining novel, *A Start in Life*, and their story unfolds in a lawyer's office run by Monsieur Desroches, a man who is still poor but is mercilessly ambitious and excessively strict. He has just hired a very young man, Oscar Husson, and welcomes him by saying that in his offices everyone "works day and night." Oscar has a garret room above the offices, and lives under the watchful eye of the chief clerk, Godeschal. Godeschal is as strict as his employer but is exposed to other aspects of life thanks to his sister, Mariette, a beautiful soloist at the ballet who lives in a world of parties. The clerk watches over the young man all the more closely because he is aware of the dangers of Paris life. The agreement Oscar has with Desroches allows him enough time to study at the School of Law, but his daily routine is formidable. He is up at five o'clock in the morning, sustains himself with a cup of coffee, and sets to work; after work he goes to his classes and occasionally to the law courts for a case, then comes home to dine with his employer and Godeschal. They eat a large dish of meat, vegetables, salad, and Gruyère cheese—the modest dessert of the young and impoverished. Once a month he has lunch with his uncle, and from time to time a friend of his mother's takes him to dinner in Palais-Royal.

This is a sad existence for a young man who dreams of beautiful clothes, dancing girls, actresses, and delicious food. Oscar has to imagine exquisite dishes to console himself for the slender daily fare, but he is not alone in this . . . the clerks have come up with a tradition: when a new clerk arrives he has to provide his colleagues with a lavish meal. To give him some idea of what is expected, they hand Oscar a dusty old compendium in which details of all the previous newcomer feasts have been recorded. It is of course a joke. The compendium is indeed old (it was found at a secondhand paper merchant's, "left about in the dust, on the stove . . . and thus it obtained a moldiness to delight an antiquarian . . . and broken corners that looked as though the rats had gnawed them"), but the recorded accounts are imaginary. At first, the new boy quakes at the thought of providing such a costly dinner, then grasps that all he need do is write out his dream menu in the book. What then do these hungry young stomachs dream of? The report of Oscar's supposed reception dinner gives us an idea. And—a touching addition on the young man's part—he invents the fact that the feast is prepared by his mother.

This day, Monday, November 25th, 1822, after a session held yesterday in the rue de la Cerisaie, Arsenal quarter, at the house of Madame Clapart, mother of the candidate-basochien Oscar Husson, we, the undersigned, declare that the repast of admission surpassed our expectations. It was composed of radishes, pink and black, gherkins, anchovies, butter and olives for hors-d'oeuvre; a succulent soup of rice, bearing testimony to maternal solicitude, for we recognized therein a delicious taste of poultry; indeed, by acknowledgment of the new member, we learned that the giblets of a fine stew prepared by the hands of Madame Clapart herself had been judiciously inserted into the family soup-pot with a care that is never taken except in such households.

Item: the said giblets inclosed in a sea of jelly.
Item: a tongue of beef with tomatoes, which rendered us all tongue-tied automatons.
Item: a compote of pigeons which caused us to think the angels had had a finger in it.
Item: a timbale of macaroni surrounded by chocolate custards.
Item: a dessert composed of eleven delicate dishes, among which we remarked (in spite of the tipsiness caused by sixteen bottles of the choicest wines) a compote of peaches of august and mirobolant delicacy.

The wines of Roussillon and those of the banks of the Rhone completely effaced those of Champagne and Burgundy. A bottle of maraschino and another of kirsch did, in spite of the exquisite coffee, plunge us into so marked an oenological ecstasy that we found ourselves at a late hour in the Bois de Boulogne instead of our domicile, where we thought we were; and Jacquinaut, the youngest clerk, aged fourteen, engaged in conversation with some well-to-do ladies of fifty-seven, thinking—from the way they behaved—they were women of easy virtue.

Now that is Balzac's idea of gastronomic paradise, a paradise derived from "a mother's care." Balzac was over forty when he wrote this novel, and had apparently still not recovered from his own mother's coldness. For once, he describes a meal that is exceptional for the care that has been put into preparing it (even saying that angels watched over the most delicious dishes), but has no element of excess apart from its eleven desserts. We notice, yet again, the inclusion of a timbale of macaroni with sweet accompaniments, and it would not be a work of Balzac's without a special mention of wonderful fruit, in this instance a compote of peaches, and an astonishing assortment of wines and liqueurs. Everything Balzac loathes about feasts—the destruction of the beautifully presented table, the inane conversations, drunkenness, and the weight of the meal on digestion—has disappeared. What remains is the tender hand that prepared the meal. Lastly, the hoax is just a harmless joke. It merely emphasizes the clerks' camaraderie and the high spirits of youth.

Nothing will ever be as good as such imaginary delights, but these employees do have an opportunity to enjoy a real feast at Le Rocher de Cancale, one of those Pantagruelian meals that lasts over six hours. The feast is paid for by a new recruit, Georges Marest, who is wealthier than his colleagues, but the whole affair ends in disaster. Oscar, our hero, eats to satisfy his hunger but drinks far more than is reasonable. Without really knowing how, he ends up in the rooms of a beautiful courtesan, Florentine, a friend of Mariette's, and there he gambles with and loses money entrusted to him by his employer. He collapses on a sofa and falls into a deep sleep, only to wake to the horror of realizing he will have lost his position.

Dreaming of meals, like dreaming of women, helps us cope with a great deal of privation. Balzac knew a thing or two about this, using this form of consolation in his long weeks of fasting and virtue. In the same way that this man did not eat when he wrote about food, writing about love and making it did not necessarily go hand in hand. Balzac refers to very diverse and extravagant forms of love. His novels are peopled by lesbians, homosexual men, old men cramming themselves with aphrodisiac pills, impetuous young boys, pure young girls, depraved women, brides wounded on their wedding night, and married women who expediently delay the moment of capitulation. There is even an officer who couples with his pet panther. It is almost a surprise that there is no necrophilia in his work. Violent love and platonic love, conjugal love and guilty love, are evoked in all their ardor, yet Balzac lived, if not chastely, at least without much splendor or variety. Two of his mistresses were the same age as his mother; he slept with his housekeeper, who was no great beauty, and he adored Madame Hanska from afar. It could therefore be said that he specialized in imaginary love, and these imaginary loves have their place here because they are always associated with food.

A YOUNG PEACH, A SOUFFLÉ, AND A TOWERING DESSERT

Through the ages, culinary delights and amorous pleasures have been connected, the one often naturally leading to the other, occasionally by means of some artificial assistance, notably large quantities of oysters. Balzac does not really believe in this natural succession. If the hefty Baron Nucingen needs to bolster his wavering powers, he swallows a couple of mysterious pills whose effects do not last very long. If Madame Jules, the sad heroine of *Ferragus*, wants to seduce her husband, she steeps herself in a fragrant bath, and later lets her coiling black hair fall over her curvaceous shoulders that are scarcely covered by her skimpy peignoir; it never occurs to her to offer him a glass of alcohol or some unusual sweetmeat.

This is because, to Balzac, no food, not even the most exquisite, is a prelude to love. Flaubert, Maupassant, and Zola had very different views—in their work, the transition from table to bed is ever present.

Maupassant depicts this route most delectably in *Bel-Ami*, during the dinner that brings together the Forestier couple, the enticing Clothilde de Marelle, and the handsome and ambitious Georges Duroy. A run through the menu is enough to create a languorous atmosphere: the oysters are "pretty and fat, like small ears, wrapped in shells, and melt between the tongue and palate like salted sweets, then a trout as pink as a young girl's skin, light tender lamb cutlets resting on a thick bed of asparagus tips." Of course they drink champagne, "and thoughts of love, slowly, invasively, came to them, gradually intoxicating their souls like clear wine falling drop by drop in their throats, warming their blood and clouding their minds." Need I explain how the evening ends? One thing is for sure, once the irreparable has been committed between Georges and Clothilde, there will be no more talk of fruit or vegetables. But during the course of an often tumultuous affair, Clothilde will try to whip up Georges's curiosity and sustain some tension in their relationship by organizing what she calls boys' escapades in disreputable establishments. One evening, sitting at a rather dirty table in a place that has a smell of frying fish hanging in the air, she orders cherries in eau-de-vie, looking around her with excitement in her eyes. "Every cherry she swallowed made her feel she had committed a sin, every drop of the peppery burning liquid running down her throat afforded her pungent pleasure, the joy of wicked and forbidden enjoyment." These lines show a perfect concordance between the two appetites. In Flaubert's *Madame Bovary*, we deduce Emma's latent sexuality when he describes her licking droplets of curaçao from her glass, and we find the same process in Zola's work.

In *The Kill*, would Renée—the high-strung young woman always looking for new sources of excitement—have succumbed to her stepson if they had not first had a late supper in a private room where he usually takes his mistresses? There he orders "the Wednesday evening menu," in other words the menu kept for his female companions, a collation of oysters and partridges. Renée asks him to send away the headwaiter, embarrassed by his watchful eye: "She was thirty but the years fell away during the escapade. She moved lithely, was a touch feverish, and this private room, this intimacy with a young man in all the hubbub of the streets, aroused her, made her look like a young girl . . . a delectable whiff of debauchery hung over the damask-clad table, and there were little quivers of pleasure in Renée's slender hands as she shifted them from her fork to her knife, her glass to her plate. She drank white wine without water, although she usually drank water barely coloured with red wine." The headwaiter comes back to clear the table, and his good-mannered composure irritates Renée, who sends him away again. Maxime then locks the door to ensure they are left in peace . . . and she surrenders on the sofa. The sequence of oysters, white wine, then embraces happens spontaneously, but where the gastronomical prelude in Maupassant's book is fresh, cheerful, and tempting, the fare eaten by Zola's incestuous couple seems banal and insipid. This first meal is a premonitory sign. Georges and Clothilde's relationship lasts, despite Georges's overweening selfishness, quite simply because they so enjoy being in bed together, while Renée's affair ends in madness. Another coupling over food involves the butcher Quenu and the beautiful Lisa in Zola's *Belly of Paris*. When they are apprentices together, "their hands sometimes met in the midst of minced meat. She sometimes helped him, holding sausage skins in her chubby hands while he stuffed them with meats and smoked bacon. Or they tasted raw sausage meat together . . . The blazing fire flushed their skin. Nothing in the world would have stopped him stirring the fatty mixture as it thickened over the heat while she solemnly debated whether or not it was cooked." As might be expected, they form a calm unified couple, a comfortable marriage between two "fatties," and the drama begins when a "skinny" erupts into their lives.

The route Balzac takes is different. It is not fruit that leads to women but women, or rather the desire aroused by women, that leads to fruit. One of the most striking sequences in *The Human Comedy,* the ball scene from *The Lily of the Valley*, illustrates this sort of osmosis. The very young Félix de Vandenesse is sent by his parents to represent the family at a ball held in Tours to celebrate Louis XVIII's return to power. Lost in the crowd, dazed by the noise, and battered by exhaustion, he has taken refuge on the edge of a bench seat when a woman sits down next to him. Thinking he is asleep, she turns her back on him. Her perfume revives him, then he notices her shoulders, "white rounded shoulders that made me long to bury my face in them, shoulders faintly pink, as if they were blushing to find themselves bare for the first time, bashful shoulders with a soul of their own and a satin skin shining in the light like a silken fabric. Between these shoulders ran a furrow which my eyes, bolder than my hand, glided into. My heart beat as I stood up to look over them, and I was entirely captivated by a bosom modestly covered with gauze, perfect in roundness, and bluely veined as it lay softly bedded in lace frills." What does he do when this beauty is revealed to him? He lunges at her back and presses himself against it, kissing her beautiful shoulders. As we would expect, the woman shrinks from the young mad-man, and he stays there motionless, "savoring the apple he has just stolen." The taste of that apple will have an influence on both their lives. Félix is young and inexperienced but we find the same assimilation between a desire for a piece of fruit and for a woman in an old rake such as Lupeaulx.

In *Bureaucracy*, the Comte des Lupeaulx, an incorrigible seducer and secretary general to the Ministry of Finance, is furiously courting the wife of one of his heads of department, the beautiful Madame Rabourdin, and comes to surprise her at home one morning. She escapes to her bedroom when he steps into the premises, but he has the affront to follow "the handsome figure, so piquant did she seem to him in her disha-bille. There is something indescribably alluring to the eye in a portion of flesh seen through an hiatus in the undergarment, more attractive by far than when it rises gracefully above the circular curve of the velvet bodice, to the vanishing line of the prettiest swan's-neck that ever a lover kissed before a ball. When the eye dwells on a woman in full dress making exhibition of her magnificent white shoulders, do we not fancy that we see the elegant dessert of a grand dinner? But the glance that glides through the disarray of muslins rumpled in sleep enjoys, as it were, a feast of stolen fruit glowing between the leaves on a garden wall."

The simmering Lupeaulx will not, however, achieve his end. Madame Rabourdin's virtue is like "a towering dessert that no one dares cut with a knife." So where Félix feels intoxicated by an apple, Lupeaulx, the experienced and somewhat offhand Parisian, can of course appreciate fruit but needs the complexity of an impressive culinary masterpiece to set him aquiver.

Sometimes Balzac does not even use the intermediary of a character. It is as if the distinction between a lovely piece of fruit and a pretty woman occasionally escapes him, and he palpitates with as much longing for a juicy pear as a glimpsed cleavage. His imaginary paradise is like the Garden of Earthly Delights, where fruit and women are two of the many temptations. But first their presentation must be perfect.

In matters of seduction, what nature provides is not always enough, as is proved by the contrast between Madame Marneffe and Baroness Hulot. The first "was like a luscious fruit coquettishly served in a handsome dish, and making the knife-blade long to be cutting it." She could be mistaken for one of Carême's masterpieces, one of those complex and refined creations that he alone could make with his secret "condiments, his spices and knowledge," while the lovely Adeline Hulot, a worthy and virtuous woman, does not know how to serve up her white bosom on a magnificently embroidered dish. There is no doubting that she would like to learn in order to win back her husband, but the poor innocent creature is not inventive enough and is too well behaved to win the game. She is about as surprising as an eel pâté or boiled meat without parsley, while the other woman is "the pepper, the spice, the alcohol in a golden goblet."

This reveals the fact that, although Balzac is convinced that sexual desire is a drive comparable to hunger, he does add an important caveat to this comparison: "A piece of bread and a carafe of water will satisfy the hunger of any man," even the most epicurean, but "the caprices of the soul are more numerous, more bewitching, more exquisite in their intensity than the caprices of gastronomy." Here we are back with the frugal Balzac who has little interest in what things taste like but is fascinated by the connection between these two appetites. He establishes it comically in *The Physiology of Marriage* and dramatically in *The Lily of the Valley*: rejecting physical love means rejecting life as wholeheartedly as refusing food.

In his letters to Madame Hanska, which were often hastily written and even rather slapdash, there are endless incidents of "I'm hungry for you, thirsty for you, could eat you"; in his books, lovers are always famished for their idol, and young girls—whose virginal complexion is adorned with "the delicate down of a young peach"—always taste like honey with their first kiss. He becomes less predictable in his humorous demonstrations of how culinary science is used by husbands who feel threatened by dreadful bachelors constantly lying in wait, "the lion of the Gospel seeking whom [they] may devour."

How can culinary science improve a husband's lot? Balzac devotes all his attention as a cynical old bachelor to this question (we should remember that he did not marry until the year he died). Age plays in a husband's favor because the young are carefree and in a hurry: "Young lovers are like hungry men; kitchen odors will not appease their hunger; they think too much of what is coming to care for the means that bring it." In other words, they are selfish lovers and therefore not gratifying. But a husband, even the most knowing in the field, has a handicap: he joins his wife in the marital bed every night, and to maintain her tender feelings, he must use all his powers to fight off familiarity. One essential principle is that "each night ought to have its menu," and there is no question of starting with the dessert because "the progression of pleasures is from the distich to the quatrain, from the quatrain to the sonnet, from the sonnet to the ballad, from the ballad to the ode, from the ode to the cantata, from the cantata to the dithyramb. The husband who commences with dithyramb is a fool." However, it is an unwise husband who uses his knowledge of love to keep his wife in a state of constant excitement. The sensible man will know how to guide her—after the fiery flames of love—toward the "temperate regions of conjugal affection." He therefore needs to know how to extinguish the fire that has blazed in the hearth, for there is nothing more reassuring for a husband than calm after the storm of physical sensations. Hence the need, at times, to keep her in a state of languor; this is where culinary science plays its part. First, our novelist advises, measure out her food and never fight the theory that we keep our figures by eating small amounts. Fresh, odorless vegetables (such as cucumber), melon, lettuce, and purslane, as well as "those tinted fruits, that coffee, that fragrant chocolate, those oranges, the golden apples of Atalanta, the dates of Arabia and the biscuits of Brussels, a wholesome and elegant food," will drain her of any dangerous vigor. And, most importantly, "refrain from affronting her delicate stomach and her refined palate by making chyle out of coarse lumps of beef, and enormous collops of mutton" (for readers without degrees in culinary science, it is worth explaining that chyle is a fluid produced in the small intestine during digestion). Over-energetic mutton should be replaced by chicken fillets, and she must certainly not be allowed to drink water! All would be lost. Why? Apparently, water evokes movement and therefore stirs desire, "with one hand holding her dress up all the way to the knee." A wife should drink water slightly colored with a pleasant-tasting Burgundy wine, but one with no virtues as a tonic; any other wine would be undesirable, except for champagne, the only wine a woman can drink and remain elegant.

It would be tempting to see this whole line of argument as a joke, if there were no equally surprising health and beauty tips in his letters to his beloved. She should eat only dark roasted meat, he decreed, a stipulation that contradicted his recommendation of chicken fillet for ladies. He also suggested— more reasonably—that she should moderate her consumption of jam and sugared almonds, both stimulants that should be treated with caution. With no explanation, he forbade her to drink coffee with cream, or even tea. True, he constantly cursed the effects that coffee, which he overused when he was working, had on his stomach, and wrote at length about the benefits of milk, oil, and lemons on the hair and complexion. He recommended washing one's face with lemon juice in the mornings and not wiping it off, and to do the same with milk at nighttime.

"When you go to bed at night, wash your forehead and temples with a small amount of thick, almost creamy milk and afterwards leave a fine layer of it applied with a finger, like cold cream; they say that this simple precaution erases wrinkles that have already formed, leaving the skin perfectly fresh, and halting the ravages of time. This discovery, my dear

Eve, is owed to a nun, like the fact that applying olive oil to hair roots stops hair graying . . . which is owed to a nun from Genoa. It will not stop wrinkles in advanced years; but it ensures freshness for another ten years, that is all; and ten more years of youth is not to be sniffed at, even though you are lovely as you are," he concluded gallantly. All these preoccupations clearly show that—in his view—food, beauty, luxury, and love are connected.

He proved this incontrovertibly by allowing a female character who refuses carnal love to die of hunger. This is the tragedy of Henriette de Mortsauf, the lady with the lovely shoulders from *The Lily of the Valley*, mentioned at the beginning of this chapter. His choice of the name Henriette was not without significance: it was the name of the Duchesse de Castries, who had allowed Balzac to court her most pressingly but "never gave him what she had promised."

Madame de Mortsauf—the tragic heroine of Balzac's most complex novel and wife of a difficult, sickly, probably syphilitic man—is not, however, a flirt or a tease. She is virtuous and devout, qualities that do not necessarily lead to happiness, neither her own nor other people's. Young Félix has been passionately in love with her since the night of the ball, and she receives him into her family home, Clochegourde, a château in Touraine. She never mentions the episode of his overly aggressive kisses and refuses to admit how much the memory still disturbs her, but welcomes him into her inner circle. He gradually settles in: the irascible husband is tamed, the children adore him, and he makes the lovely Henriette's life easier. But she forces him into the role of oldest child, forbidding him any lover's words or gestures. He is permitted only the language of flowers, and he makes up symbolic bouquets for her in which above the "white tufts peculiar to a Sedum that grows in the vineyards of Touraine, a faint image of the wished-for forms, bowed like a submissive slave-girl . . . A grand red double poppy stands up with bursting buds, flaunting its burning flame above starry jessamine and above the ceaseless shower of pollen." She understands their significance full well but is happy to accept them.

He complies with her wishes: they have an extremely intense relationship, made painful by the lack of outlet. Just once she succumbs to a tender impulse, granting him the casual form of address, *tu* instead of *vous*; it is a vocal caress. It is during the grape harvest, a time of plenty and abundance, "the happy dessert of the harvested feast." The house is full of people and provisions. In a generous, well-maintained household such as Madame de Mortsauf's, the grape harvesters are amply fed, and their good humor bears witness to this. The girls are cheerful and full of laughter, the men carrying casks sing brightly through the day, knowing the evenings will be good to them. Félix and the children join in the party and celebrations, fill their baskets with beautiful bunches of grapes, and run to show them off to Madame de Mortsauf. It is at this point that, treating him as her child, "stroking my hair and my neck, she gave me a little slap on the cheek, adding 'You're soaking!,'" using the familiar *tu* form. But Félix knows she will go no further, that she will not allow herself to be affected by the amorous mood pervading all the young people around them, by the "Bacchic form" of the last fine days of the season. He turns back into the rows of vines and abandons himself to the "ineffable pleasure of a physical employment." He remarks, "I learned how much wisdom comes of labour and I understood monastic rule." He may understand it but he does not adopt it.

Félix moves away, leaving the "angel" behind to start a career in Paris, and there he meets the ultimate tigress, Lady Dudley. This Englishwoman is not timid: "She craved for spice, for pepper to feed her heart on, as English epicures insist on pungent condiments to revive their palate . . . [L]ike a lioness that has carried her prey in her mouth and brought it to her den to devour," she throws herself at the young man. He lets himself be loved, discovers new pleasures, but does not renounce the divine Henriette, or at least that is what he believes, in his male innocence. But everyone knows about everything in Balzac's world. Henriette hears of his liaison thanks to a deliberate indiscretion of her own mother's, and is struck down into an alarmingly despondent state. Félix runs to her side and sees her; in some consternation he realizes that the magnificent woman-fruit of the novel's opening "had the look of fruit on which bruises are beginning to show, and which has turned prematurely yellow from the ravages of a worm within." Her eyes are dry and disturbingly shiny, like the straw-colored tint of her forehead. She greets him coldly, but cannot contain her distress or her curiosity about Lady Dudley for long, knowing that the latter has deprived herself of her own children and braved society's conventions to give herself entirely to Félix. In her realization of this woman's audacity, her "world seemed to be upside down; her ideas were in confusion. Startled by the magnitude of this idea, suspecting that happiness might justify this immolation, hearing within her the outcries of the rebellious flesh, she stood aghast, gazing at her spoilt life." The revelation continues. In her innocence, she has thought Félix would remain faithful to her, that he would have "the virtue of a priest" or of the unfortunate Monsieur de Mortsauf, who has been kept away from the marital bed and whose virtuous wife grants not the least sign of tenderness (she is too stupid to think of any, the husband confesses to the young man with a flash of anger).

Balzac defended himself against Madame Hanska's jealousy by impressing on her that prolonged chastity reduced men to imbecility. Félix is more dramatic, declaring that "the heart, bereft of the nourishment it needs, feeds on itself and sinks into exhaustion, which is not death, but which leads to it. Nature cannot be persistently cheated." He does not know how right he is. Nature is about to reassert its rights over Henriette with a violence that proves fatal.

The young man returns to his duties to the king in Paris. A few months pass before he suddenly hears that Madame de Mortsauf is dying. He asks for leave and hurries to Clochegourde. On the way to the château he meets the doctor who confirms the news: "she is dying aged and pinched by hunger, for she will die of starvation. For the last forty days the stomach is closed as it were, and rejects every kind of food in whatever form it is given." The doctor is perfectly aware that she is dying of sorrow but cannot think why. Her suffering seems to be a fine illustration of Monsieur de Mortsauf's theory that "all our emotions converge on the gastric centres," a theory that in happier times made Félix reply with a smile that this meant "people of strong feeling die of indigestion."

In fact, it is not so much Félix's infidelity that is killing her as raging frustration that he never suspected how much she desired him, and never overcame her virtuous resistance. She is dying from the revelation that the most fundamental thing in life slipped through her fingers thanks to her obstinate rejection of love. Balzac—who associates hunger and thirst in their most instinctive and most brutal form with being deprived of love's joys and gratifications—puts these words into the starving, dying woman's mouth the last time she sees the man she has always loved: "Yes, I will live . . . is it possible that I should die, I who have not lived?" And through the open window she hears the hubbub of the grape harvest, and cries: "Félix, the vintagers are going to dinner and I, the mistress of the house, am starving . . . It is the same with love, they are happy; they are happy!"

$\mathcal{B}$ALZAC BROUGHT meals into literature, in all their diversity. Digressions about the price of a cup of coffee, about how boring an eel pâté could be, about the consolations offered by a fat carp or what could be gained from interpreting how a table of food was set out would have been unthinkable before him. After him, Flaubert, Zola, Maupassant, and then Proust went on to incorporate meals and gastronomy in their novels, each in his own way. Flaubert—who was from Normandy and once wrote to his mistress, Louise Colet, with a surge of loving enthusiasm, "I've never loved you so much, I had oceans of cream in my heart"—used meals at length to depict rural hospitality during Emma's wedding celebrations, the crushing boredom of the Bovary household, and, in *A Sentimental Education*, the contrast between the placid Madame Arnoux and the highly strung Rosanette. Maupassant was the master of lovers' intimate meals and rural feasting. Zola intoxicated himself with the abundance and beauty of raw ingredients in *The Belly of Paris*, the novel that he devotes entirely to food. Proust, like Balzac, completes the portrait of various women who are mistress of their house— be it the Duchesse de Guermantes, Madame Verdurin, Odette Swann, or the narrator's mother—by describing the care they put into laying out a meal; on the other hand, he allows himself to highlight the comedy of pompous service in the pages devoted to Balbec's restaurant. But he was better than anyone else at giving certain foods a poetic dimension. Surely only Proust could have seen a multicolored cathedral in the blue and pink veins of the fish laid before him. Balzac had thrown the doors wide open for him.

Notes

INTRODUCTION

4 *"is like milk . . ."*
Honoré de Balzac, *Modeste Mignon,* in *Modeste Mignon and Other Stories*, trans. Clara Bell (Philadelphia: Gebbié Publishing, 1898), 27.

4 *"It is good wine . . ."*
Ibid., 172.

5 *"like a barrel of lard . . ."*
Guy de Maupassant, *Boule de Suif* (Ball of Lard), Collection Folio Classique (Paris: Gallimard, 1973), 36. Excerpt translated by Adriana Hunter.

5 *"the bland smell of salmon . . ."*
Émile Zola, *Le Ventre de Paris* (The Belly of Paris), Bibliothèque de la Pléiade, I (Paris: Gallimard, 1960), 739. Excerpt translated by Adriana Hunter.

7 *"[His] lips quivered . . ."*
Léon Gozlan, *Balzac en pantoufles* (Paris: Maisonneuve et Larose, 2001), 26. Excerpt translated by Adriana Hunter.

8 *"knew nothing of caresses . . ."*
André Maurois, *Prométhée ou La vie de Balzac* (Paris: Hachette, 1965), 14. Excerpt translated by Adriana Hunter.

10 *"The famous rillettes and rillons . . ."*
Honoré de Balzac, *The Lily of the Valley,* in *"The Lily of the Valley," "The Firm of Nucingen," "The Country Doctor," and Other Stories,* trans. James Waring (Boston: Dana Estes, 1901), 5–6.

11 *"a sort of appetite . . ."*
Balzac, *Louis Lambert,* in *"Seraphita" and Other Stories,* vol. 4 of *The Novels and Dramas of Honoré de Balzac,* trans. Clara Bell (New York: Croscup and Holby, 1905), 146.

11 *"He was struck down . . ."*
Laure Surville, *Balzac, sa vie et ses œuvres* (Paris: L'Harmatan, 2005), 21. Excerpt translated by Adriana Hunter.

13 *"Monsieur Balzac is kindly requested . . ."*
Maurois, *Prométhée,* 40. Excerpt translated by Adriana Hunter.

14 *"diverse bits of bread . . ."*
Balzac, *Colonel Chabert,* in *The Works of Honoré de Balzac,* Athenaeum Edition, vol. 2, trans. Katherine Prescott Wormeley (New York: Athenaeum Club, 1896), 7.

14 *"oilcloth which covers the long table . . ."*
Balzac, *Father Goriot,* in *The Novels and Dramas of Honoré de Balzac: "Father Goriot" and Other Stories,* vol. 26, trans. Ellen Marriage and James Waring (New York: Croscup and Holby, 1905), 6.

16   *"I once used to live . . ."*
Balzac, *Facino Cane*, in *"The Member for Arcis," "The Seamy Side of History," and Other Stories*, trans. Clara Bell (Boston: Dana Estes, 1901), 325.

16   *"kept by her in blinkers . . ."*
Balzac, *Cousin Betty*, trans. James Waring (London: J.M. Dent, 1897), 229.

17   *"a woman's caresses scare away . . ."*
Ibid., 231.

17   *"to avoid wearying the brain . . ."*
Balzac, *Lettres à Madame Hanska*, ed. Robert Laffont (Paris: Bouquins, 1990), 1:337. Excerpt translated by Adriana Hunter.

18   *"a goose and a bit of chicory . . ."*
Ibid., 2: 400.

18   *"eats aimlessly, stupidly, soullessly . . ."*
Balzac, *Physiologie gastronomique* (Paris: Ollendorf, 1902), 156. Excerpt translated by Adriana Hunter.

19   *"in three or four Gargantuan mouthfuls . . ."*
Gozlan, *Balzac en pantoufles*, 52. Excerpt translated by Adriana Hunter.

19   *"knowing, subtle, divine decoction . . ."*
Ibid., 28.

20   *"Father Socquard simply boiled . . ."*
Balzac, *The Peasantry*, in *The Country Parson and The Peasantry*, trans. Ellen Marriage (Boston: Dana Estes, 1901), 282.

20   *"ideas swing into action . . ."*
Balzac, *Traité des excitants modernes* (Paris: Ollendorf, 1902), 82. Excerpt translated by Adriana Hunter.

23 *"sumptuousness beyond reason . . ."*
Balzac, *Lettres à Mme Hanska*, 1: 200. Excerpt translated by Adriana Hunter.

26 *"His work table, his bed . . ."*
Ibid., 1: 313. Excerpt translated by Adriana Hunter.

27 *"Despite the prison's rules . . ."*
Edmond Werdet, *Portrait intime de Balzac* (Paris, 1879), 253. Excerpt translated by Adriana Hunter.

28 *"laborers, masons, painters . . ."*
Balzac, *Lettres à Mme Hanska*, 1: 459. Excerpt translated by Adriana Hunter.

28 *"I won't name any names . . ."*
Gozlan, *Balzac en pantoufles*, 27. Excerpt translated by Adriana Hunter.

30 *"in our house, we will never . . ."*
Balzac, *Lettres à Mme Hanska*, 1: 869.

II PARIS AT MEALTIMES

40 *"If the French have as great an aversion . . ."*
Honoré de Balzac, Honorine, in *"The Atheist's Mass" and Other Stories*, trans. Clara Bell (London: J.M. Dent, 1896), 21.

40 *"as Borel . . . elaborates it . . ."*
Ibid., 22.

42 *"As soon as a stomach arrives in Paris . . ."*
C. Gardeton, quoted by Jean-Paul Aron in *La sensibilité alimentaire* (Paris: Librairie Armand Colin, 1967), 19. Excerpt translated by Adriana Hunter.

43   *"went to Very's and ordered dinner . . ."*
Balzac, *Lost Illusions*, in *A Distinguished Provincial at Paris: "Lost Illusions" and Other Stories*, trans. Ellen Marriage (Philadelphia: Gebbie Publishing, 1899), 19–20.

45   *"the officer on duty had to shoo away street children"*
Emmanuel de Waresquiel, *Cent jours: La tentation de l'impossible, mars–juillet 1815* (Paris: Fayard, 2008), 356.

48   *"My dear Master . . ."*
Revue d'Histoire Littéraire de la France, October–December 1953: 479. Excerpt translated by Adriana Hunter.

48   *"the beauty of each piece . . ."*
Jean-Paul Aron, *Le mangeur du XIXème siècle* (Paris: Laffont, 1973), 50. Excerpt translated by Adriana Hunter.

49   *"drank like a fish . . ."*
Balzac, *The Girl with the Golden Eyes*, in *"The Thirteen," "Father Goriot," and Other Stories*, trans. Ellen Marriage (Boston: Dana Estes, 1901), 323.

49   *notary clerks gather here*
Balzac, *A Start in Life*, in *"La Comédie Humaine" of Honoré de Balzac: "A Start in Life" and Other Stories*, trans. Katharine Prescott Wormeley (Boston: Little, Brown, 1896), 312.

49   *"quite in his element [there] . . ."*
Balzac, *Lost Illusions*, 12.

49   *"waiters, whom a provincial . . ."*
Balzac, *Cousin Betty*, trans. James Waring (London: J.M. Dent, 1897), 429.

51 *"she liked anything amusing . . ."*
Balzac, *The Collection of Antiquities,* in *The Works of Honoré de Balzac: "Béatrix," "The Jealousies of a Country Town" and "The Commission in Lunacy,"* trans. Ellen Marriage (Philadelphia: Avil Publishing, 1901), 212.

52 *"ravishing women walked through the dining room . . ."*
Balzac, *Cousine Bette,* (Paris, Édition Furne, 1848), 336. Excerpt translated by Adriana Hunter.

53 *"four bottles of Vouvray . . ."*
Fernand Lotte, "Balzac et la table," Année Balzacienne, 1962: 120. Excerpt translated by Adriana Hunter.

53 *"costly guest"*
Balzac, *Traité des excitants modernes,* in *Oeuvres diverses* (Paris: Ollendorf, 1902), 2: 72. Excerpt translated by Adriana Hunter.

55 *"narrow streets, dark and muddy . . ."*
Balzac, *A Harlot's Progress,* vol. 1., trans. James Waring (London: J. M. Dent, 1896), 21.

55 *"a dirty, poky, disreputable street . . ."*
Balzac, *Gambara* in *Comédie Humaine: A Father's Curse and Other Stories,* trans. James Waring (London: J. M. Dent, 1898), 183.

56 *"anyone who was anyone crossed . . ."*
Balzac, "Le diable à Paris," in *Histoire et physiologie des boulevards de Paris* (Paris, 1853). Excerpt translated by Adriana Hunter.

56 *"The boulevards are now to Paris . . ."*
Ibid.

59 *The provincial guest makes the mistake*
Balzac, *The Unconscious Mummers and Other Stories,* trans. Ellen Marriage (London: J.M. Dent, 1897), 4.

59 *"in the course of which they consumed . . ."*
Ibid., 4.

61 *"'Dearest heart,' said she . . ."*
Balzac, *The Muse of the Department*, in *"A Prince of Bohemia" and Other Stories*, trans. James Waring and J.N.O. Rudd (Philadelphia: Gebbie Publishing, 1899), 154.

65 *"Where we stopped . . ."*
Léon Gozlan, *Balzac en pantoufles* (Paris: Maisonneuve et Larose, 2001), 150. Excerpt translated by Adriana Hunter.

66 *"on the uppers of his boots . . ."*
Balzac, *Lost Illusions*, 157.

67 *"table napkin slipped through a numbered . . ."*
Ibid., 47.

67 *"There a dinner of three courses . . ."*
Ibid.

67 *"The fare is not very varied . . ."*
Ibid., 49.

69 *"Few Parisian restaurants are so well worth seeing . . ."*
Ibid., 4–5.

71 *"and a smell of cooking, lamp oil and tobacco . . ."*
Gustave Flaubert, *L'éducation sentimentale* (Paris: Gallimard, Pléiade, 1952), 15. Excerpt translated by Adriana Hunter.

72 *"a place where the sound of wheels . . ."*
Balzac, *Father Goriot*, in *The Novels and Dramas of Honoré de Balzac: "Father Goriot" and Other Stories*, vol. 26, trans. Ellen Marriage and James Waring (New York: Croscup and Holby, 1905), 2–3.

74 *"Arrived in the Rue Neuve-Sainte-Geneviève. . ."*
Ibid., 82.

75 *"all stereotyped by novel writers . . ."*
Balzac, *A Harlot's Progress*, vol. 1, 263.

III   GREAT OCCASIONS

78 *"the circumscribed saturnalias . . ."*
Honoré de Balzac, *The Magic Skin*, in *The Works of Honoré de Balzac: "The Magic Skin," "The Quest of the Absolute," and Other Stories*, trans. Ellen Marriage (Boston: Dana Estes, 1901), 38.

78 *"The rooms were adorned with silk and gold . . ."*
Ibid., 42–43.

78 *"each paid his tribute of admiration . . ."*
Ibid., 44.

79 *"the damask linen marked 'A, B, C' . . ."*
Balzac, *An Old Maid*, in *"La Comédie Humaine" of Honoré de Balzac: "The Two Brothers"; "An Old Maid,"* trans. Katharine Prescott Wormeley (Boston: Little, Brown, 1899), 504–505.

79 *"a damask cloth that is dazzlingly white"*
Balzac, *Ferragus*, in *Ferragus: Chief of the Dévorants; The Last Incarnation of Vautrin*, trans. Katharine Prescott Wormeley (Boston: Roberts Brothers, 1895), 75.

83 *"royal profusion"*
Balzac, *The Magic Skin*, 44–45.

83 *"Everyone ate as he spoke . . ."*
Ibid.

84 *"tall statuettes . . . sustained and carried . . ."*
Ibid., 54–55.

85 *"fiery sparks" of champagne*
Ibid., 45.

85 *"The pyramids of fruit were ransacked . . ."*
Ibid., 55.

93 *"The guests were punctual . . ."*
Balzac, *The Rise and Fall of César Birotteau*, trans. Ellen Marriage (London: J. M. Dent, 1896), 173.

93 *"the morass of chill reality"*
Ibid., 182.

94 *"where the traditions of grandeur . . ."*
Balzac, *Father Goriot*, in *The Novels and Dramas of Honoré de Balzac: "Father Goriot" and Other Stories*, vol. 26, trans. Ellen Marriage and James Waring (New York: Croscup and Holby, 1905), 121.

94 *"The dessert was like a squadron after a battle . . ."*
Balzac, *The Red Inn*, in *The Works of Honoré de Balzac*, Athenaeum Edition, vol. 17, trans. Katharine Prescott Wormeley (New York: Athenaeum Club, 1896), 177.

95 *"You are surprised as you enter the room . . ."*
Balzac, *Gobseck*, in *A Woman of Thirty, A Forsaken Lady, La Grenadière, The Message, Gobseck*, trans. Ellen Marriage (London: J.M. Dent, 1897), 336–337.

97 *"swoop down on the pastries and truffled fowl . . "*
Émile Zola, *La Curée* (The Kill), Pléiade I (Paris: Gallinard, 1960), 250–251. Excerpt translated by Adriana Hunter.

102   *"the surest thermometer for gauging the income of a Parisian family . . ."*
Honoré de Balzac, *Cousin Betty*, trans. James Waring (London: J.M. Dent, 1897), 64.

104   *"veined with blue and yellow . . ."*
Émile Zola, *Le Ventre de Paris*, Bibliothèque de la Pléiade, I (Paris: Gallimard, 1960), 427. Excerpt translated by Adriana Hunter.

104   *"had to choose between ten mustards . . ."*
Gustave Flaubert, *L'éducation sentimentale*, 78. Excerpt translated by Adriana Hunter.

104   *"cultivated all the mail coach drivers . . ."*
Ibid., Excerpt translated by Adriana Hunter.

104   *"The tyranny of the palate . . ."*
Balzac, *Cousin Pons*, trans. Ellen Marriage (London: J.M. Dent, 1897), 13.

105   *"she herself cooked 'to amuse herself '"*
Balzac, *Pierrette*, in *"Pierrette" and "The Abbé Birotteau,"* trans. Clara Bell (London: J.M. Dent, 1896), 41.

106   *"the dining-room, badly kept by the single servant . . ."*
Balzac, *Cousin Betty*, 63.

106   *"served and eaten in cracked plates . . ."*
Ibid., 63–64.

106   *"live in comfort on [a] narrow income"*
Balzac, *The Country Doctor*, in *"The Lily of the Valley," "The Firm of Nucingen," " The Country Doctor," and Other Stories*, trans. Ellen Marriage and Clara Bell (Boston: Dana Estes, 1901), 198.

107   *"in every household the plague of servants . . ."*
Balzac, *Cousin Betty*, 175–176.

107   *"domestic robber, a thief taking wages . . ."*
Ibid.

108   *"So she had brought from the depths . . ."*
Ibid., 176.

109   *When Balzac was planning to hire*
Balzac, *Lettres à Madame Hanska*, ed. Robert Laffont (Paris: Bouquins, 1990), 2:792.

110   *"of slums which are, as it were, the entrails of Paris . . ."*
Balzac, *The Rise and Fall of César Birotteau*, trans. Ellen Marriage (London: J. M. Dent, 1896), 98–99.

112   *"entered [their] service without effects . . ."*
Balzac, *Petty Troubles of Married Life*, in *"The Physiology of Marriage"; "Petty Troubles of Married Life": Repertory of the "Comédie Humaine,"* trans. J. Walker McSpadden (Boston: Dana Estes, 1901), 395.

115   *"expressing a complicity of satirical thoughts"*
Balzac, *The Lesser Bourgeoisie*, trans. Katharine Prescott Wormeley (Boston: Roberts Brothers, 1896), 211.

116   *"The soup was a rather pale bouillon . . ."*
Ibid., 108–109.

119   *"Lending a hand to her two servants . . ."*
Ibid., 125.

120   *"by tuning his clarionet . . ."*
Ibid., 126–127.

122 *"in Paris people eat [half-heartedly] . . ."*
Balzac, *An Old Maid*, in *"La Comédie Humaine" of Honoré de Balzac: "The Two Brothers"; "An Old Maid,"* trans. Katharine Prescott Wormeley (Boston: Little, Brown, 1896), 479.

122 *"fat Rhine carp with a sauce . . ."*
Balzac, *Cousin Pons*, 61.

123 *"turn you out a simple dish of beans . . ."*
Balzac, *A Harlot's Progress*, in *La Comédie Humaine*, vol. 1, trans. James Waring (London: J.M. Dent, 1896), 66.

123 *"In the provinces, the lack of occupation . . ."*
Balzac, *The Black Sheep* [*La rabouilleuse*], trans. George B. Ives (Philadelphia: George Barrie and Son, 1897), 227–228.

124 *"dishes well known in the country . . ."*
Balzac, *The Peasantry*, in *The Country Parson and The Peasantry*, trans. Ellen Marriage (Boston: Dana Estes, 1901), 44.

124 *"miser full of tender cares . . ."*
Ibid., 219.

124 *"his fashion of blowing the fire . . ."*
Ibid., 218.

125 *"the mattresses were of the best . . ."*
Ibid., 222.

125 *"Dinner, breakfast, and supper alike . . ."*
Ibid., 226–227.

126 *"exaggeratedly wide mouth and thin lips . . ."*
Ibid., 225–226.

127 *"was the very pattern of a working housekeeper . . ."*
Balzac, *The Country Doctor*, 32–33.

128 *"A woman whom every one obeys . . ."*
Ibid., 31.

128 *"it would have been a sad thing . . ."*
Ibid., 32.

128 *must have known that Louis XIV's horticulturalist*
Susan Pinkard, *A Revolution in Taste* (Cambridge, U.K.: Cambridge University Press, 2009), 74.

129 *"peculiar kind of damask linen invented . . ."*
Ibid., 138–139.

132 *"The dining-room, paved in black and white stone . . ."*
Balzac, *An Old Maid*, 437.

132 *"Mariette remarked to the chief-justice . . ."*
Ibid., 469–470.

135 *"In Paris people . . . trifle with their pleasure . . ."*
Ibid., 479.

V THE MISERS AND THE FOOD WORSHIPPERS

138 *"in twenty-five years Graslin had not so much . . ."*
Honoré de Balzac, *A Country Parson*, in *The Country Parson and The Peasantry*, trans. Ellen Marriage (Boston: Dana Estes, 1901), 21.

140 *"the vanilla was replaced by burned oats . . ."*
Balzac, The Black Sheep [La rabouilleuse], trans. George B. Ives (Philadelphia: George Barrie and Son, 1897), 270.

141 *"Monsieur Hochon rose . . ."*
Ibid., 271.

144 *"sometimes flew into a rage . . ."*
Balzac, *Gobseck*, in *A Woman of Thirty, A Forsaken Lady, La Grenadière, The Message, Gobseck*, trans. Ellen Marriage (London: J.M. Dent, 1897), 312.

144 *"There was a flush in his pale cheeks . . ."*
Ibid., 343.

145 *"he swallows it all and is none the fatter . . ."*
Ibid., 371.

145 *"the childishness and incomprehensible obstinacy of age . . ."*
Ibid., 374.

146 *"take what you like; help yourself . . ."*
Ibid., 372.

146 *"a quantity of eatables of all kinds . . ."*
Ibid., 373.

153 *"'That warms me!' he muttered . . ."*
Balzac, *Eugénie Grandet* from *Eugénie Grandet, Ursule Mirouët, and Other Stories*, trans. Ellen Marriage and Clara Bell (Boston: Dana Estes, 1901), 184.

153 *"[i]n matters financial M Grandet . . ."*
Ibid., 9.

154 *"Women eat little at a formal dinner . . ."*
Balzac, *Petty Troubles of Married Life*, in *"The Physiology of Marriage"; "Petty Troubles of Married Life": Repertory of the "Comédie Humaine,"* trans. J. Walker McSpadden (Boston: Dana Estes, 1901), 376–377.

156 *"Suppose that conjugal misfortune . . ."*
Balzac, *The Physiology of Marriage*, in *"The Physiology of Marriage"*;

"Petty Troubles of Married Life": Repertory of the "Comédie Humaine," trans. J. Walker McSpadden (Boston: Dana Estes, 1901), 304.

157   "she strains [his favorite brew] with special care . . ."
Ibid., 305.

158   "contrived to display new virtues . . ."
Balzac, *Béatrix*, in *"La Comédie Humaine" of Honoré de Balzac: "Béatrix" and "A Commission in Lunacy,"* trans. Katharine Prescott Wormeley (*Boston: Little, Brown,* 1899), 376.

159   "would motion to the servants . . ."
Ibid., 354.

159   "consort[ed] with Madame de Rochefide's cook . . ."
Ibid.

160   "Indian sauces they serve in England in cruets . . ."
Ibid., 354–355.

160   "the food was exquisite . . ."
Balzac, *Albert Savarus*, in *The Country Parson and The Peasantry*, trans. Ellen Marriage (Boston: Dana Estes, 1901), 272.

161   "The ferocious hunger familiar to convalescents . . ."
Balzac, *The Message*, in *"About Catherine De'Medici" and Other Stories*, trans. Clara Bell (Philadelphia: Gebbie Publishing, 1900), 392.

161   "among the gilded and insolent youth . . ."
Balzac, *Father Goriot*, in *The Novels and Dramas of Honoré de Balzac: "Father Goriot" and Other Stories*, vol. 26, trans. Ellen Marriage and James Waring (New York: Croscup and Holby, 1905), 35.

162   "had few pleasures left . . ."
Ibid., 121.

162 *"the luxury of style and that of content"*
Ibid.

163 *"in the time of the Restoration . . ."*
Ibid.

163 *"officers who took part in them . . ."*
Ibid., 121–122.

164 *"malicious, evil-minded old man"*
Balzac, *The Black Sheep* [*La rabouilleuse*], trans. George B. Ives (Philadelphia: George Barrie and Son, 1897), 202.

165 *"in the flower of old age"*
Ibid., 211.

165 *"nature had foiled the schemes of his lust"*
Ibid., 215.

165 *"as an Eastern slave would have done"*
Ibid., 213.

165 *"the hellish round of hunger and everlasting toil"*
Ibid.

166 *"He is renowned at Issoudun . . ."*
Ibid., 228.

167 *"'What do you suppose that old ape means to do . . .'"*
Ibid., 212–213.

168 *"Mademoiselle Brazier [Flore] . . ."*
Ibid., 240.

168 *"the brain is atrophied . . ."*
Balzac, *Cousin Pons*, trans. Ellen Marriage (London: J.M. Dent, 1897), 17.

169 *"walking along the Boulevard des Italiens . . ."*
Ibid., 1.

170 *"tender, dreamy, sensitive soul"*
Ibid., 16.

170 *"much as barristers note down the cases . . ."*
Ibid., 12

170 *"a countenance which was flattened . . ."*
Ibid., 4.

170 *"Plenty of men are doomed to this fate . . ."*
Ibid., 16–17.

171 *"times of the Empire when Paris . . ."*
Ibid., 13.

172 *"being three times as old"*
Balzac, *Le Cousin Pons*, Pléiade (Paris: Gallimard, 1950), 189. Excerpt translated by Adriana Hunter.

172 *"much as they accepted the taxes"*
Balzac, *Cousin Pons*, 15.

172 *"Alas! A shudder ran through him . . ."*
Ibid., 14.

173 *"[H]e became a kind of harmless, well-meaning spy . . ."*
Ibid.

173 *"Pons contracted the only marriage . . ."*
Balzac, *Le Cousin Pons*, 537. Excerpt translated by Adriana Hunter.

174 *"that heart and stomach were at war . . ."*
Balzac, *Cousin Pons*, 21.

174 *"A stomach thus educated is sure to react . . ."*
Ibid., 13.

175 *"Brillat-Savarin has deliberately set himself to justify . . ."*
Ibid., 17.

177 *"And very soon, in spite of all that Schmucke could do . . ."*
Ibid., 60.

178 *"A single symptom will throw light . . ."*
Ibid., 60–61.

179 *"The dishes were a rapture to think of! . . ."*
Ibid., 82–83.

180 *"The amount of wine, German and French . . ."*
Ibid., 83.

183 *"left about in the dust, on the stove . . ."*
Balzac, *A Start in Life*, in *"A Marriage Settlement" and Other Stories*, trans. Clara Bell (London: J.M. Dent, 1897), 197–198.

183 *"This day, Monday, November 25th . . ."*
Ibid., 202–203.

VI A YOUNG PEACH, A SOUFFLÉ,
    AND A TOWERING DESSERT

190 *"pretty and fat, like small ears . . ."*
Guy de Maupassant, *Bel-Ami* (Paris: Albin Michel, 1966), 97. Excerpt translated by Adriana Hunter.

190 *"and thoughts of love, slowly, invasively, came to them . . ."*
Ibid., 99.

191   *"Every cherry she swallowed made her feel . . ."*
Ibid., 119.

191   *"She was thirty but the years fell away . . ."*
Émile Zola, *Le Curée*, Pléiade I (Paris: Gallimard, 1960), 451–452.
Excerpt translated by Adriana Hunter.

192   *"their hands sometimes met . . ."*
Zola, *Le Ventre de Paris*, Bibliothèque de la Pléiade, I (Paris: Gallimard, 1960), 649. Excerpt translated by Adriana Hunter.

193   *"white rounded shoulders that made me long to bury my face in them . . ."*
Honoré de Balzac, *The Lily of the Valley*, in *"The Lily of the Valley," "The Firm of Nucingen," "The Country Doctor," and Other Stories*, trans. James Waring (Boston: Dana Estes, 1901), 18.

194   *"the handsome figure, so piquant did she seem . . ."*
Balzac, *Bureaucracy*, in *"La Comédie Humaine" of Honoré de Balzac: "Bureaucracy," "Secrets of the Princesse de Cadignan," "Unconscious Comedians," "Pierre Grassou,"* trans. Katharine Prescott Wormeley (Boston: Little, Brown, 1899), 228–229.

195   *"a towering dessert that no one dares cut . . ."*
Ibid.

195   *"was like a luscious fruit coquettishly served . . ."*
Balzac, *Cousin Betty*, trans. James Waring (London: J.M. Dent, 1897), 194.

196   *"a piece of bread and a carafe of water . . ."*
Balzac, *The Physiology of Marriage*, in *"The Physiology of Marriage"; "Petty Troubles of Married Life": Repertory of the "Comédie Humaine,"* trans. J. Walker McSpadden (Boston: Dana Estes, 1901), 43.

196   *"the caprices of the soul are more numerous . . ."*
Ibid.

196 *"the delicate down of a young peach"*
Ibid., 19.

197 *"the lion of the Gospel seeking . . ."*
Ibid., 44.

197 *"Young lovers are like hungry men . . ."*
Balzac, *Béatrix*, in *"La Comédie Humaine"* of Honoré de Balzac: *"Béatrix"* and *"A Commission in Lunacy,"* trans. Katharine Prescott Wormeley (Boston: Little, Brown, 1899), 192.

197 *"each night ought to have its menu"*
Balzac, *The Physiology of Marriage*, 64.

197 *"the progression of pleasures is from the distich . . ."*
Ibid.

198 *"temperate regions of conjugal affection"*
Balzac, *A Daughter of Eve*, in *"La Comédie Humaine"* of Honoré de Balzac: *"Modeste Mignon,"* *"A Daughter of Eve,"* *"The Peace of a Home,"* trans. Katharine Prescott Wormeley (Boston: Little, Brown, 1899), 33.

198 *"those tinted fruits, that coffee, that fragrant chocolate . . ."*
Balzac, *The Physiology of Marriage*, 136.

198 *"refrain from affronting her delicate stomach . . ."*
Ibid.

198 *"with one hand holding her dress up . . ."*
Balzac, *La Physiologie du Mariage*, 136 (Paris: Edition Furne, 1848), 452. Excerpt translated by Adriana Hunter.

199 *"when you go to bed at night . . ."*
Balzac, *Lettres à Madame Hanska*, ed. Robert Laffont (Paris: Bouquins, 1990), 1: 863. Excerpt translated by Adriana Hunter.

200   *"never gave him what she had promised"*
André Maurois, *Prométhée ou La vie de Balzac* (Paris: Hachette, 1965), 213. Excerpt translated by Adriana Hunter.

201   *"white tufts peculiar to a Sedum . . ."*
Balzac, *The Lily of the Valley*, 96–97.

201   *"the happy dessert of the harvested feast"*
Balzac, *Le Lys dans la vallée*, Pléiade (Paris: Gallimard, 1961), 861. Excerpt translated by Adriana Hunter.

202   *"stroking my hair and my neck . . ."*
Balzac, *The Lily of the Valley*, 100.

202   *"Bacchic form"*
Ibid.

202   *"ineffable pleasure of a physical employment"*
Ibid.

202   *"I learned how much wisdom comes of labour . . ."*
Ibid., 101.

202   *"She craved for spice . . ."*
Ibid., 194.

203   *"had the look of fruit . . ."*
Ibid., 202.

203   *"world seemed to be upside down . . ."*
Ibid., 207.

204   *"the heart, bereft of the nourishment it needs . . ."*
Ibid., 208.

204   *"she is dying aged and pinched by hunger . . ."*
Ibid., 244.

204 *"all our emotions converge on the gastric centres . . ."*
Ibid., 200.

204 *"people of strong feeling die of indigestion"*
Ibid.

205 *"Yes, I will live . . ."*
Ibid., 255.

205 *"Félix, the vintagers are going to dinner . . ."*
Ibid.

205 *"I've never loved you so much . . ."*
Gustave Flaubert, *Correspondance* (Paris: Conard, 1927), iv, 27.

CREDITS

Grateful acknowledgment is given to the following for permission to reproduce photographs. For cases where only a secondary source is given, every effort has been made to identify the copyright holder(s) of the image.

13 Portrait of Honoré de Balzac, oil on canvas, by the French School, Musée de la Ville de Paris, Maison de Balzac, Paris, France. Giraudon / The Bridgeman Art Library

21 Napier patent coffee machine, c.1845. Private collection / Photo © Bonhams, London, UK / The Bridgeman Art Library

24 Madame Hanska, lithograph, engraved by Emile Lassalle after a painting by Jean Francois Gigoux, Musée de la Ville de Paris, Maison de Balzac, Paris, France. Giraudon / The Bridgeman Art Library

34 Middle-class Boardinghouse, color engraving, caricature, 1881, by Lavrate, Musée de la Ville de Paris, Musée Carnavalet, Paris, France. Archives Charmet / The Bridgeman Art Library

39 Engraving from *Le Mangeur du XIXe siècle* by Jean-Paul Aron (Paris: Éditions Robert Laffont, 1973).

44 Engraving from *Le Mangeur du XIXe siècle* by Jean-Paul Aron (Paris: Éditions Robert Laffont, 1973).

56 Le Boulevard des Italiens by Edmond Georges Grandjean. Private Collection / Photo © Christie's Images / The Bridgeman Art Library

60 Engraving from *Le Mangeur du XIXe siècle* by Jean-Paul Aron (Paris: Éditions Robert Laffont, 1973).

73 The Vauquer Boarding House, from *Le Père Goriot*, engraving, 1900, by Albert Lynch, Musée de la Ville de Paris, Maison de Balzac, Paris, France. Archives Charmet / The Bridgeman Art Library

80 Engraving from Urbain Dubois, nineteenth century. From the 1965 edition of *Le Grand Dictionnaire de Cuisine* by Alexandre Dumas, published by Claude Tchou.

95 Engraving from *Le Mangeur du XIXe siècle* by Jean-Paul Aron (Paris: Éditions Robert Laffont, 1973).

98 Engraving from Urbain Dubois, nineteenth century. From the 1965 edition of *Le Grand Dictionnaire de Cuisine* by Alexandre Dumas, published by Claude Tchou.

110 Les Halles, color lithograph, 1893, by Leon Lhermitte, Musée de la Ville de Paris, Musée Carnavalet, Paris, France. Archives Charmet / The Bridgeman Art Library

150 Engraving from *Le Mangeur du XIXe siècle* by Jean-Paul Aron (Paris: Éditions Robert Laffont, 1973).

162 The Oyster Eaters, lithograph, 1825, by Louis-Léopold Boilly. From the 1965 edition of *Le Grand Dictionnaire de Cuisine* by Alexandre Dumas, published by Claude Tchou.

ANKA MUHLSTEIN was born in Paris in 1935. She has published biographies of Queen Victoria, James de Rothschild, Cavelier de La Salle, and Astolphe de Custine; a study on Catherine de Médicis, Marie de Médicis, and Anne of Austria; a double biography, *Elizabeth I and Mary Stuart;* and an essay on Manhattan. Her latest book, *Mr. Proust's Library,* a slim volume on Proust as a reader, will be published by Turtle Bay Press in 2012. She has won two prizes from the Académie Française and the Goncourt Prize for Biography. She and her husband, Louis Begley, have written a book on Venice, *Venice for Lovers.* They live in New York.

~~~~~~

ADRIANA HUNTER studied French and Drama at the University of London. She has translated over forty books including works by Agnès Desarthe, Amélie Nothomb, Frédéric Beigbeder, Véronique Ovaldé, and Catherine Millet, and has been short-listed for the Independent Foreign Fiction Prize twice. She lives in Norfolk, England.